DATE DUE

Self-Mutilation

Other Books of Related Interest:

At Issue Series

Cosmetic Surgery

Body Piercing and Tattoos

"Congress shall make no law ... abridging the freedom of speech, or of the press."

First Amendment to the U.S. Constitution

The basic foundation of our democracy is the First Amendment guarantee of freedom of expression. The Opposing Viewpoints series is dedicated to the concept of this basic freedom and the idea that it is more important to practice it than to enshrine it.

Self-Mutilation

Mary E. Williams, Book Editor

GREENHAVEN PRESS

An imprint of Thomson Gale, a part of The Thomson Corporation

THOMSON
─────✲─────™
GALE

Detroit • New York • San Francisco • New Haven, Conn. • Waterville, Maine • London

THOMSON

™

GALE

Christine Nasso, *Publisher*
Elizabeth Des Chenes, *Managing Editor*

© 2008 The Gale Group.

Star logo is a trademark and Gale and Greenhaven Press are registered trademarks used herein under license.

For more information, contact:
Greenhaven Press
27500 Drake Rd.
Farmington Hills, MI 48331-3535
Or you can visit our Internet site at http://www.gale.com

LIBRARY OF CONGRESS CATALOGING-IN-PUBLICATION DATA

Self-mutilation / Mary E. Williams, book editor.
  p. cm. -- Opposing Viewpoints
 Includes bibliographical references and index.
 ISBN-13: 978-0-7377-3828-5 (hardcover)
 ISBN-13: 978-0-7377-3829-2 (pbk.)
 1. Self-mutilation. I. Williams, Mary E., 1960-
 RC552.S4S457 2008
 616.85'82--dc22

                                                          2007028156

ISBN-10: 0-7377-3828-6
ISBN-10: 0-7377-3829-4

Printed in the United States of America
10 9 8 7 6 5 4 3 2 1

Contents

Chapter 3: What Triggers Self-Mutilation?

Chapter 4: What Should Be Done to Reduce Self-Injurious Behavior?

Why Consider
Opposing Viewpoints?

"The only way in which a human being can make some approach to knowing the whole of a subject is by hearing what can be said about it by persons of every variety of opinion and studying all modes in which it can be looked at by every character of mind. No wise man ever acquired his wisdom in any mode but this."

John Stuart Mill

In our media-intensive culture it is not difficult to find differing opinions. Thousands of newspapers and magazines and dozens of radio and television talk shows resound with differing points of view. The difficulty lies in deciding which opinion to agree with and which "experts" seem the most credible. The more inundated we become with differing opinions and claims, the more essential it is to hone critical reading and thinking skills to evaluate these ideas. Opposing Viewpoints books address this problem directly by presenting stimulating debates that can be used to enhance and teach these skills. The varied opinions contained in each book examine many different aspects of a single issue. While examining these conveniently edited opposing views, readers can develop critical thinking skills such as the ability to compare and contrast authors' credibility, facts, argumentation styles, use of persuasive techniques, and other stylistic tools. In short, the Opposing Viewpoints series is an ideal way to attain the higher-level thinking and reading skills so essential in a culture of diverse and contradictory opinions.

In addition to providing a tool for critical thinking, Opposing Viewpoints books challenge readers to question their own strongly held opinions and assumptions. Most people form their opinions on the basis of upbringing, peer pressure, and personal, cultural, or professional bias. By reading carefully balanced opposing views, readers must directly confront new ideas as well as the opinions of those with whom they disagree. This is not to simplistically argue that everyone who reads opposing views will—or should—change his or her opinion. Instead, the series enhances readers' understanding of their own views by encouraging confrontation with opposing ideas. Careful examination of others' views can lead to the readers' understanding of the logical inconsistencies in their own opinions, perspective on why they hold an opinion, and the consideration of the possibility that their opinion requires further evaluation.

Evaluating Other Opinions

To ensure that this type of examination occurs, Opposing Viewpoints books present all types of opinions. Prominent spokespeople on different sides of each issue as well as well-known professionals from many disciplines challenge the reader. An additional goal of the series is to provide a forum for other, less-known, or even unpopular viewpoints. The opinion of an ordinary person who has had to make the decision to cut off life support from a terminally ill relative, for example, may be just as valuable and provide just as much insight as a medical ethicist's professional opinion. The editors have two additional purposes in including these less-known views. One, the editors encourage readers to respect others' opinions—even when not enhanced by professional credibility. It is only by reading or listening to and objectively evaluating others' ideas that one can determine whether they are worthy of consideration. Two, the inclusion of such viewpoints encourages the important critical thinking skill of objectively evaluating an author's credentials and bias. This evaluation will illuminate an author's reasons for taking a particular stance on an issue and will aid in readers' evaluation of the author's ideas.

It is our hope that these books will give readers a deeper understanding of the issues debated and an appreciation of the complexity of even seemingly simple issues when good and honest people disagree. This awareness is particularly important in a democratic society such as ours in which people enter into public debate to determine the common good. Those with whom one disagrees should not be regarded as enemies but rather as people whose views deserve careful examination and may shed light on one's own.

Thomas Jefferson once said that "difference of opinion leads to inquiry, and inquiry to truth." Jefferson, a broadly educated man, argued that "if a nation expects to be ignorant and free . . . it expects what never was and never will be." As individuals and as a nation, it is imperative that we consider the opinions of others and examine them with skill and discernment. The Opposing Viewpoints series is intended to help readers achieve this goal.

David L. Bender and Bruno Leone,
Founders

Introduction

"The act of self-injury provides a way to manage intolerable feelings or a way to experience some sense of feeling."

—Cornell Research Program on Self-Injurious Behavior

At age twelve, Ann of Buffalo, New York, felt inundated by the pressures of life. Her beloved grandfather had recently died. Because of an illness, she had missed nearly half a year of school, and she was struggling to keep up with her studies. She had also just been placed in a new school, where she was having trouble making friends. For reasons that she could not articulate, Ann began to make shallow cuts on her arms and legs with a razor blade, drawing a few drops of blood at a time.

Four years later, at age sixteen, Ann recalled her years of self-cutting in the April 22, 2007, *Buffalo News*: "I became addicted. . . . The bigger a problem I had, the more I would cut myself. Sometimes I was just punishing myself. Sometimes I just used it to help me forget about my other problems."

Referred to variously as "self-mutilation," "deliberate self-harm" (DSH), "self-injurious behavior" (SIB), "self-inflicted violence" (SIV), or "cutting," self-harm includes a broad range of behaviors in which an individual inflicts injury on his or her body for purposes that are not socially sanctioned and without suicidal intent. Self-harm includes, among other actions: intentional cutting, scratching, or carving of the skin; punching and bruising of the body; pulling, ripping or burning of the skin or hair; breaking bones, and swallowing toxic substances. A few analysts controversially argue that body piercing, tattooing, and extensive plastic surgery may qualify as forms of self-mutilation as well.

Psychiatric researcher Armando Favazza classifies four major forms of self-injurious behavior: major, stereotypic, compulsive, and impulsive. Major and stereotypic self-harm, seen among people with severe psychiatric disorders, is relatively rare. Compulsive and impulsive forms of self-injury are more common and more likely to be found among adolescent and young adult populations. Compulsive self-injury, which includes nail biting, hair pulling, and scratching of the skin is commonly linked to obsessive-compulsive disorder. Impulsive self-injury, most often expressed through skin cutting, burning, and carving, is associated with depression, anxiety, an abusive past, post-traumatic stress disorder, and borderline personality disorder, although it is not necessarily indicative of a mental disorder.

Discussions about self-mutilation usually focus on Favazza's fourth category: impulsive self-injury. Recent research gathered from hospitals, clinics, and private physicians indicates that this form of self-harm is on the rise. One study in the *Journal of Abnormal Psychology* claims that from 14 to 39 percent of adolescents engage in self-injurious behavior. In a recent study of 728 college students in Canada, psychologist Nancy Heath found that 12 percent had tried self-injury at least once during high school. Other more conservative estimates put the figure at 6 percent. But most experts seem to agree that the problem has grown over the past decade. "Every clinician says it's increasing," says Michael Hollander, a director of a Massachusetts outpatient clinic that treats cutters. "I've been practicing for thirty years, and I think it's gone up dramatically."

Why do some people engage in self-injury? Self-harmers themselves report a variety of reasons for this behavior, but most would agree that it is rooted in emotional torment. Some self-injurers are in so much emotional turmoil that they find physical pain to be a release; others who are in a dissociative "numbed-out" state injure themselves in order to feel

something, even if it's painful. Cutting also releases endorphins—the body's natural pain relievers—creating a "high"
that can become addictive. As self-injury expert Deb Martinson maintains, "when people who self-injure get emotionally
overwhelmed, an act of self-harm brings their levels of psychological and physiological tension back to a bearable base-
line level almost immediately. In other words, they feel a
strong uncomfortable emotion, don't know how to handle it
(indeed, often do not have a name for it), and know that
hurting themselves will reduce the emotional discomfort extremely quickly. . . . This explains why self-injury can be so
addictive: It works. When you have a quick, easy way to make
the bad stuff go away for a while, why would you want to go
through the hard work of finding other ways to cope? Eventually, though, the negative consequences add up, and people do
seek help."

Some analysts believe that the recent increase in self-injury
is partly due to its trendy "glamour factor." Celebrities including Angelina Jolie, Fiona Apple, and Christina Ricci have admitted to past self-mutilation. While these confessions can encourage self-injurers to seek help for their problem—other
youths may feel tempted to emulate an admired celebrity. Syn-
dicated columnist Michelle Malkin maintains that "this mad-
ness would not be as popular as it is among young people if
not for the glamorizing endorsement of nitwit celebrities." As
Malkin explains, celebrity quotes about self-injurious behavior
are often repeated on Web sites about cutting, increasing the
self-harm "contagion" factor. Some youths even form "cutting
clubs" to engage in self-injury with others or to compare stories about their wounds.

Most self-injury takes place in private, however, with self-
harmers going to great lengths to keep their behavior a secret.
Thus the first big step for a repeat self-injurer is to come forward and talk about their problem with friends, parents, teachers, and counselors. It's in secrecy that painful wounds thrive,

experts note. But once self-injurers share their painful burden with others and learn healthier coping strategies, they eventually stop wounding themselves. *Opposing Viewpoints: Self-Mutilation* explores both the causes of and several solutions to this disconcerting problem in the following chapters: How Serious a Problem Is Self-Mutilation? Does Body Modification Constitute Self-Mutilation? What Triggers Self-Mutilation? What Should Be Done to Reduce Self-Injurious Behavior? The authors in this volume offer a variety of perspectives on this distressing—and often misunderstood—behavior.

OPPOSING
VIEWPOINTS®
SERIES

CHAPTER 1

How Serious a Problem Is Self-Mutilation?

Chapter Preface

Self-injury, self-harm, and self-inflicted violence are the phrases most commonly used to describe the actions of those who deliberately hurt themselves in a way that causes tissue damage to the body. Self-injury can take many forms, including cutting the skin with sharp objects; burning, slapping, or punching one's body; hitting a heavy object; picking at scabs until they bleed; pulling out hair; and biting oneself. Cutting, burning, and headbanging are the most common forms of self-injury among adolescents.

Deliberate self-harm, especially among youths, is understandably anxiety-provoking for the parents and loved ones of a self-injurer. The discovery of slash marks or scars on a friend's wrists, for example, might cause alarm and arouse concerns about suicide. Indeed, as suicide is the result of a grievously self-harming act, it seems logical to conclude that self-inflicted wounds are signs of unsuccessful suicide attempts. However, researchers often assert that most self-injurers do not commit suicide. As child psychiatrist Sidhartha Hakim points out, "Deliberate self-harming is roughly 100 times more common than completed suicide in childhood or adolescence."

There are certain correlations between self-harm and suicide. For example, youths who self-harm and youths who have suicidal thoughts share several traits in common, including higher than normal levels of anxiety and depression, problems with parents, self-blaming thoughts, and low self-esteem. Those who self-harm or have suicidal thoughts are more likely to have friends who self-harm or have suicidal thoughts—and they also believe that they have fewer people in whom they can confide as compared with others.

But while self-injurers have an increased risk of suicide when compared with non-self-injurers, only 0.5 percent of self-harmers commit suicide, reports adolescent psychiatrist Xavier Pommereau. Self-cutting, the most common form of self-injury among teens, is rarely accompanied by the desire to kill oneself. In fact, self-inflicted cuts are usually intentionally superficial—not deep enough to cause life-threatening bleeding. Experts point out that self-injury is most often an attempt to cope with or relieve painful or hard-to-express emotions. According to the National Self-Harm Network, for many youths self-injury may serve as a survival strategy and a way to avert suicide.

Self-injury should be taken seriously, however, as it indicates an inability to cope with overwhelming feelings in a healthy way. As the contributors to the following chapter point out, in certain cases self-injury is a symptom of a mental disorder that requires medical treatment, and some people find self-injury addictive and engage in it repeatedly. While most self-injurers are not suicidal, their actions still deserve attention and concern.

> *"With all the talk about it, cutting can almost seem like the latest fad. But cutting is a serious problem."*

Self-Cutting Is a Serious Problem

D'Arcy Lyness

Self-injury is an unhealthy way of coping with emotional difficulties and personal pain, explains D'Arcy Lyness in the following viewpoint. While it is not a very common behavior, some people see it as a fad because of the public attention it has recently received. But self-harm, which often takes the form of cutting, is not simply a trend—it is a serious problem that might be a sign of mental illness and that can result in serious physical injury. Self-cutters should seek out help so that they can learn healthier ways of managing the problems that led to their injurious behavior, the author concludes. Lyness, a child and adolescent psychologist in Wayne, Pennsylvania, is the behavioral health editor for the KidsHealth Web site.

As you read, consider the following questions:

1. In the author's view, why do some youths think that cutting makes them seem daring or grown-up?

2. What is an "unhealthy coping mechanism," according to Lyness?

3. What commonly triggers teenagers to start cutting themselves, in Lyness's opinion?

Emma's mom first noticed the cuts when Emma was doing the dishes one night. Emma told her mom that their cat had scratched her. Her mom seemed surprised that the cat had been so rough, but she didn't think much more about it.

Emma's friends had noticed something strange as well. Even when the weather was hot, Emma wore long-sleeved shirts. She had become secretive, too, like something was bothering her. But Emma couldn't seem to find the words to tell her mom or her friends that the marks on her arms were from something that she had done. She was cutting herself with a razor when she felt sad or upset.

What Is Cutting?

Injuring yourself on purpose by making scratches or cuts on your body with a sharp object—enough to break the skin and make it bleed—is called cutting. Cutting is a type of self-injury, or SI. Cutting is more common among girls, but guys sometimes self-injure, too. People may cut themselves on their wrists, arms, legs, or bellies. Some people self-injure by burning their skin with the end of a cigarette or lighted match.

When cuts or burns heal, they often leave scars or marks. People who injure themselves usually hide the cuts and marks and sometimes no one else knows.

Self-injury is not new. It's also not a very common behavior. But lately people are talking about it more. As guys and girls hear about cutting, they may feel curious about it and why people do it. Because it seems a little bit forbidden, some younger teens may think that cutting might make them seem daring, grown up, or popular.

With all the talk about it, cutting can almost seem like the latest fad. But cutting is a serious problem.

Why Do People Cut Themselves?

It can be hard to understand why people cut themselves on purpose. Cutting is what experts call an unhealthy coping mechanism. This means that the people who do it have not developed healthy ways of dealing with strong emotions, intense pressure, or upsetting relationship problems.

There are lots of good, healthy ways to cope with difficulties, such as talking problems over with parents, other adults, or friends; putting problems in perspective; and getting plenty of exercise. But people who cut haven't developed these skills. When emotions don't get expressed in a healthy way, tension can build up—sometimes to a point where it seems almost unbearable. Cutting may be an attempt to relieve that extreme tension. It's a confused way of feeling in control. That's one of the reasons why younger teens are more likely to cut.

The urge to cut might be triggered by strong feelings the person can't express—such as anger, hurt, shame, frustration, or depression. People who cut sometimes say they feel they don't fit in or that no one understands them. A person might cut because of losing someone close or to escape a sense of emptiness. Cutting might seem like the only way to find relief, or the only way to express personal pain over relationships or rejection.

People who cut or self-injure sometimes have other mental health problems that contribute to their emotional tension. Cutting is sometimes (but not always) associated with depression, bipolar disorder, eating disorders, obsessive thinking, or compulsive behaviors. It can also be a sign of mental health problems that cause people to have trouble controlling their impulses or to take unnecessary risks. Some people who cut themselves have problems with drug or alcohol abuse.

Some people who cut have had a traumatic experience, such as living through abuse, violence, or a disaster. Self-injury may feel like a way of "waking up" from a sense of numbness after a traumatic experience. Or it may be a way of

Self-harm As a Way of Coping

Extreme feelings of fear, anger, guilt, shame, helplessness, self-hatred, unhappiness, depression or despair can build up over time. When these feelings become unbearable, self-harm can be a way of dealing with them.

Reasons young people have given for their self-harm include:

- When the level of emotional pressure becomes too high it acts as a safety valve—a way of relieving the tension.

- Cutting makes the blood take away the bad feelings.

- Pain can make someone feel more alive when feeling numb or dead inside.

- Punishing oneself relieves feelings of shame or guilt.

- When it's too difficult to talk to anyone, it's a form of communication about unhappiness—a way of acknowledging the need for help.

- Self-harm gives a sense of control when other parts of life may not.

National Children's Bureau,
"Young People and Self Harm," 2003.
www.selfharm.org.uk.

reinflicting the pain they went through, expressing anger over it, or trying to get control of it.

What Can Happen to People Who Cut?

Although cutting may provide some temporary relief from a terrible feeling, even people who cut agree that cutting isn't a good way to get that relief. For one thing, the relief doesn't last—the troubles that triggered the cutting remain, they're just masked over.

People don't usually intend to hurt themselves permanently when they cut. And they don't usually mean to keep cutting once they start. But both can happen. It's possible to misjudge the depth of a cut, making it so deep that it requires stitches (or, in extreme cases, hospitalization). Cuts can become infected if a person uses nonsterile or dirty cutting instruments—razors, scissors, pins, or even the sharp edge of the tab on a can of soda.

Most people who cut aren't attempting suicide. Cutting is usually a person's attempt at feeling better, not ending it all. Although some people who cut do attempt suicide, it's usually becasue of the emotional problems and pain that lie behind their desire to self-harm, not the cutting itself.

Cutting can be habit forming. It can become a compulsive behavior—meaning the more a person does it, the more he or she feels the need to do it. The brain starts to connect the false sense of relief from bad feelings to the act of cutting, and it craves this relief the next time tension builds. When cutting becomes a compulsive behavior, it can seem impossible to stop. So cutting can seem almost like an addiction. A behavior that starts as an attempt to feel more in control can end up controlling you.

How Does Cutting Start?

Cutting often begins on an impulse. It's not something the person thinks about ahead of time. Shauna says, "It starts when something's really upsetting and you don't know how to talk about it or what to do. But you can't get your mind off feeling upset, and your body has this knot of emotional pain. Before you know it, you're cutting yourself. And then somehow, you're in another place. Then, the next time you feel awful about something, you try it again—and slowly it becomes a habit."

Natalie, an eleventh grader who started cutting in middle school, explains that it was a way to distract herself from feelings of rejection and helplessness she felt she couldn't bear. "I never looked at it as anything that bad at first—just my way of getting my mind off something I felt really awful about. I guess part of me must have known it was a bad thing to do, though, because I always hid it. Once a friend asked me if I was cutting myself and I even lied and said 'no.' I was embarrassed."

Sometimes self-injury affects a person's body image. Jen says, "I actually liked how the cuts looked. I felt kind of bad when they started to heal—and so I would 'freshen them up' by cutting again. Now I can see how crazy that sounds, but at the time, it seemed perfectly reasonable to me. I was all about those cuts—like they were something about me that only I knew. They were like my own way of controlling things. I don't cut myself anymore, but now I have to deal with the scars."

You can't force someone who self-injures to stop. It doesn't help to get mad at a friend who cuts, reject that person, lecture her, or beg him to stop. Instead, let your friend know that you care, that he or she deserves to be healthy and happy, and that no one needs to bear their troubles alone.

Cutting—The New Cool?

Girls and guys who self-injure are often dealing with some heavy troubles. Many work hard to overcome difficult problems. So they find it hard to believe that there are some teens who cut just because they think it's a way to seem tough and rebellious.

Tia tried cutting because a couple of the girls at her school were doing it. They pressured her. "It seemed like if I didn't do it, they would think I was afraid or something. So I did it once, but when I walked away, I thought about how lame it was to do something like that to myself for no good reason. Next time they asked I just said, 'no thanks, it's not for me.'"

If you have a friend who suggests you try cutting, say what you think. Why get pulled into something you know isn't good for you? There are plenty of other ways to express who you are. (Not giving in to peer pressure is one of them!)

Lindsay had been cutting herself for 3 years because of abuse she suffered as a child. She's 16 now and hasn't cut herself in more than a year. "I feel proud of that," Lindsay says. "So when I hear girls talk about it like it's a fad, it really gets to me."

Getting Help

There are better ways to deal with troubles than cutting—healthier, long-lasting ways that don't leave a person with emotional and physical scars. The first step is to get help with the troubles that led to the cutting in the first place. Here are some ideas for doing that:

1. **Tell someone**. People who have stopped cutting often say the first step is the hardest—admitting to or talking about cutting. But they also say that after they open up about it, they often feel a great sense of relief. Choose someone you trust to talk to at first (a parent, school counselor, teacher, coach, doctor, or nurse). If it's too difficult to bring up the topic in person, write a note.

2. **Identify the trouble that's triggering the cutting**. Cutting is a way of reacting to emotional tension or pain. Try to figure out what feelings or situations are causing you to cut. Is it anger? Pressure to be perfect? Relationship trouble? A painful loss or trauma? Mean criticism or mistreatment? Identify the trouble you're having, then tell someone about it. Many people have trouble figur-

ing this part out on their own. This is where a mental health professional can be helpful.

3. **Ask for help.** Tell someone that you want help dealing with your troubles and the cutting. If the person you ask doesn't help you get the assistance you need, ask someone else. Sometimes adults try to downplay the problems teens have or think they're just a phase. If you get the feeling this is happening to you, find another adult (such as a school counselor or nurse) who can make your case for you.

4. **Work on it.** Most people with deep emotional pain or distress need to work with a counselor or mental health professional to sort through strong feelings, heal past hurts, and to learn better ways to cope with life's stresses. One way to find a therapist or counselor is to ask at your doctor's office, at school, or at a mental health clinic in your community.

Although cutting can be a difficult pattern to break, it is possible. Getting professional help to overcome the problem doesn't mean that a person is weak or crazy. Therapists and counselors are trained to help people discover inner strengths that help them heal. These inner strengths can then be used to cope with life's other problems in a healthy way.

*"Sitting with the urges to hurt myself
. . . can be more excruciating than the
self-injury itself."*

Not Acting on the Urge to Cut Is a Serious Problem

Alex Williams

In the following viewpoint, Alex Williams, a volunteer diagnosed with mental health problems, discusses the torment associated with her self-harming behavior. When she heeded a medical professional's warnings to stop cutting herself, she actually became more depressed because she could no longer use self-injury as an outlet for her emotional problems. Social and medical workers should be aware that self-harmers are still facing enormous challenges even when they have stopped physically injuring themselves, Williams asserts.

As you read, consider the following questions:

1. How many times did Williams visit the hospital within a recent ten-month period?
2. What did an emergency consultant say would happen to the author if she did not stop cutting herself?
3. What did Williams do to cope with the depression she faced after she stopped self-harming?

When I am in a cycle of self-harm I cannot imagine that there can be anything worse. But I have found that there is—sitting with the urges to hurt myself and not acting on them. This can be more excruciating than the self-injury itself.

In a recent 10-month period I needed 23 blood transfusions with more than 50 hospital admissions. Self-harm became my focus. I thought of myself as a self-harmer and about how much damage I had done. While I sometimes wanted to change I felt reluctant to give up the harming. It was as though it formed my identity and purpose. But the cutting had become painful. Before there had been some strong emotion overriding the pain—anger, upset or anxiety. These lessened but I continued to feel low.

Feeling Defeated

What also challenged my habitual self-harming was when an emergency consultant told me I would not be alive in six months if I continued. She warned me that my hand might have to be amputated if an infection spread. But I still felt the desire to harm myself. Being unable to do this because of unbearable physical pain made me feel defeated.

The evenings were hard to get through since I associated them with the rituals of my self-injury. I found myself thinking about harming myself all the time and was frustrated that I could not do it as I had before. I became more depressed and even neglected myself when it came to washing and dressing.

The Benefit of Support Groups

Several things have helped me through, including internet support groups. You get to know the people who frequently post messages and are there to support other members. I have often sent messages about feeling that what I am living now is just an existence and how I miss the mental drama of self-

My Self-Harm Cycle

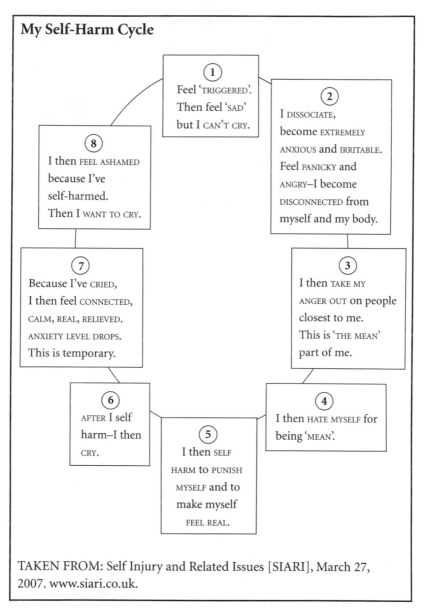

1 Feel 'TRIGGERED'. Then feel 'SAD' but I CAN'T CRY.

2 I DISSOCIATE, become EXTREMELY ANXIOUS and IRRITABLE. Feel PANICKY and ANGRY–I become DISCONNECTED from myself and my body.

3 I then TAKE MY ANGER OUT on people closest to me. This is 'THE MEAN' part of me.

4 I then HATE MYSELF for being 'MEAN'.

5 I then SELF HARM to PUNISH MYSELF and to make myself FEEL REAL.

6 AFTER I self harm–I then CRY.

7 Because I've CRIED, I then feel CONNECTED, CALM, REAL, RELIEVED. ANXIETY LEVEL DROPS. This is temporary.

8 I then FEEL ASHAMED because I've self-harmed. Then I WANT TO CRY.

TAKEN FROM: Self Injury and Related Issues [SIARI], March 27, 2007. www.siari.co.uk.

harming. You write "trigger" in the subject line of messages if they concern self-injury, abuse or suicide. I feel the support group members understand.

I joined an occupational therapy sports group and this has given me a reason to regain energy by taking iron tablets to replace lost blood. It meets weekly and is facilitated by an occupational therapist and a support worker. There are six members from both sexes. The group plays badminton and softball tennis at the local sports centre.

One practical way of getting through each day has been comfort eating. I make sure that this is done on lots of fruit and vegetables so minimising weight gain.

Social care workers should recognise that someone is battling self-harm even when they are no longer physically hurting themselves. The mental torment does not end when that person resists using the blade.

> *"The majority of children and adolescents who purposefully cut themselves do not have an immediate wish or intent to kill themselves"*

Most Self-Injurers Do Not Have an Increased Risk of Suicide

Betsy Bates

Self-cutting is not usually a precursor of suicide, writes Betsy Bates in the following viewpoint. According to child psychiatrist Michael Jellinek, cited by Bates, persistent cutting may stem from a wide range of motivations, from faddish self-expression to deep emotional disturbance. Even acutely depressed self-injurers may cut themselves in an attempt to manage inner pain and as a way to cry for help—but without intending to kill themselves, notes Bates. Family doctors should avoid overreacting to self-harming behavior—which could cause more shame and anxiety for the cutter—and uncritically assess the patient's reasons for cutting. Bates is a writer for Family Practice News.

Betsy Bates, "'Cutting' May Be More Widespread Than Imagined," *Family Practice News*, vol. 35, no. 6, March 15, 2005, p. 50. Copyright 2005 International Medical News Group. Reproduced by permission.

As you read, consider the following questions:

1. According to Michael Jellinek, quoted by the author, how are tattooing, piercing, and superficial decorative cutting related?

2. In what way is cutting a solution, rather than a problem, for self-injurers, according to Bates?

3. According to the author, what is the most helpful response a physician could have to a patient who self-injures?

Self-injurious behavior in the form of "cutting" may not be as rare as child psychiatrists once believed, nor is it always a red flag for imminent suicide.

Instead, it may be an attempt by a severely disconnected, depressed teenager to gain focus and control, said Michael Jellinek, M.D., chief of child psychiatry at Massachusetts General Hospital in Boston.

"Cutting means different things to different individuals, and it occurs in a variety of settings and circumstances. Often, it's profoundly misunderstood," Dr. Jellinek told this newspaper [*Family Practice News*].

A Variety of Motivations for Cutting

Child psychiatrists once assumed that cutting was a precursor to suicide. And although this is true in some cases—especially when self-inflicted wounds are deep and in potentially lethal locations—the majority of children and adolescents who purposefully cut themselves do not have an immediate wish or intent to kill themselves.

"I see superficial, repetitive cutting as a behavior that spans a wide spectrum of motivations, from a me-too form of self-expression to a sign of deep emotional pain and dissociation," he said.

In its most benign form, cutting is an outgrowth of a societal change in which the body is used as a template.

Is Self-Injury Attempted Suicide?

No, self-injury and suicide have an intimate relationship, but are different. Each individual has their own motivations and mix of self-injuring and suicidal feelings.

- Self-injury often represents the prevention of a suicidal period.

- Self-injury is one way of averting suicide.

- Self-injury may be a survival strategy.

- Self-injury is frequently the least possible amount of damage and represents extreme self-restraint.

National Self Harm Network,
"Self-Injury: Myths and Common Sense," 1998.
www.nshn.co.uk/facts.html.

Piercings, Tattoos, and Cutting

"As technology makes our lives more anonymous, many young people communicate their individuality by using their bodies as canvases," Dr. Jellinek said. Body piercings or tattoos may represent a spectrum of meaning that ranges from a display of fashion sense to a screaming need for recognition.

For example, piercings may be subtle, as in the piercing of an ear or navel, or extreme, as in multiple piercings involving the face, breasts, and genitals, he explained. Tattoos can be small, unobtrusive designs on the ankle or small of the back, or can constitute an aggressive, bodywide statement that is impossible to cover with clothing.

In this context, superficial decorative cutting may be the self-expression of a fairly untroubled adolescent who is copying a behavior from a more disturbed acquaintance, or a fad—and not necessarily a deviant one—that is followed by a group of friends, said Dr. Jellinek.

Cries for Attention and Help

He cited a hypothetical patient, Brian, an otherwise well-functioning teenager who, after a sad experience or while very anxious during exam time, makes small cuts on his forearm with the sharp edge of a paper clip to mimic the cutting he's witnessed in a friend with major depression. He might tell other friends about this behavior as a means of seeking reassurance or empathy.

For another hypothetical patient, Maria, cutting may arise from acute depression and self-recrimination. She may have cut herself at a moment when she felt life was not worth living, not to actually take her life but as a suicidal gesture, a cry for help, and a punishment in which the external pain is a substitute for even more overwhelming inner pain.

Meanwhile, another adolescent, Katie, may secretly cut herself in a more serious, repetitive manner. Her wounds may form a pattern. She may cut herself obsessively every day, more deeply each time, hiding scars in various stages of healing as she pulls away from friends and family, drops out of activities, and sees her grades plummet.

The Need for a Nonjudgmental Attitude

It's vital for family physicians to realize that to Brian, Maria, and especially Katie, cutting feels like a solution, not a problem.

The cutting behavior awakens Katie from a disconnected emotional state to which she escapes when she is overwhelmed by despondency, anxiety, and low self-esteem. When she cuts—or even when she experiences the physical pain of a recent wound—she feels focused, appropriately punished, and a bit more in touch with herself. Cutting is something over which she has control.

"If you discover Katie's cutting and react with horror, you will unknowingly add to her sense of shame over a behavior that is the only way she has found to relieve her emotional torment," Dr. Jellinek advised.

"Instead, if you notice injuries and explain in a nonjudgmental way that you know of teenagers who try to help themselves through difficult times by cutting, she may feel a tremendous sense of relief."

Seeing Cutting as a Solution

He recommended that family physicians take the time to explain that they're willing to help the patient try to understand why he or she has chosen cutting as a solution, and what the real problem may be.

"Let her know that you may be able to help her find other alternatives that will help her achieve the same goal: feeling connected, strong, and in control."

Dr. Jellinek characterized cutting as a highly complex symptom of deeper psychological issues. Sorting out the intrapsychic states of adolescents as they think about cutting and then cut themselves is a difficult task, even for a mental health clinician with experience and training in this area.

He tapped pediatricians and family physicians as important "first responders" who can help by being uncritical, understanding, and open to patients' explanations of their cutting behavior.

"Recognizing the cutting as a solution rather than as the whole problem is a critical first step," he said.

| *"Self-injury is itself wrongly associated with women."*

Self-Injury Affects Males as Well as Females

LifeSIGNS

Contrary to popular perception, self-injury (SI) is not limited to teenage girls, notes LifeSlGNS in the following viewpoint. Flawed research is probably responsible for this misperception, the authors point out. In today's culture, men often feel pressured to appear strong and to avoid looking needy in any way, so they are less likely to seek support when they undergo emotional distress. Thus males who self-injure as a way to cope with overwhelming emotions are far less likely to share their predicament with others. LifeSlGNS is an online self-injury guidance and support network based in the United Kingdom.

As you read, consider the following questions:

1. Why did Wedge turn to self-injury, according to Life-SIGNS?
2. In the authors' view, why is there a higher rate of suicide among young men?

LifeSIGNS, "Male Self Injury Taken Seriously," www.lifesigns.org.uk/what/male.html. *LifeSIGNS*, www.selfharm.org.uk. Reproduced by permission of LifeSIGNS, Self Injury Guidance & Network Support.

3. What kinds of people does self-injury affect, according to LifeSIGNS?

"I have always suspected that self-injury [SI] affects males as much as females," says Wedge, "and I've always been suspicious of the media when it portrays self-injury as only a teenage girl thing. I know from my experience that it is not. I started hurting myself before I was a teen, and I hurt myself the most after my teens—I am male, and I'm a confident and fairly decent bloke. I have struggled with difficult things in life though, and I have had trouble dealing with my emotional responses; I turned to SI to deal with my distress, to make the pain 'real' and to ground myself, to just cope and get on with things."

"I think there's an extent to which my experience of self-injury has been a vicious circle," says Nick. "As a man it was less socially accepted to talk about feelings, especially negative feelings that don't fit with the alpha male archetype, and so there was a need to find a different way to cope with them. For me, like many other men, this was self-injury. To make things worse self-injury is itself wrongly associated with women, so being open about my self-injury was simply not an option, which in turn led to more negative feelings and more self-injury."

Guys and Dolls

LifeSIGNS has always suspected that bias in research into SI may be responsible for the apparent predominance of females who experience it, and a recent report by M.J. Marchetto suggests that this is indeed the case:

> No gender differences were observed among skin-cutters, most of whom reported experiences of trauma. BPD [Borderline Personality Disorder] was recorded for a minority of those skin-cutters without a history of trauma. PBI [Parental Bonding Index] scores discriminated between non-BPD

skin cutters and non-BPD comparison participants without a history of trauma.... Although these results provide further confirmation of a potential association between prior trauma and repetitive skin-cutting, they rigorously challenge the validity of reported gender differences for this behaviour. Further, this study has identified that repetitive skin-cutting can arise independently of BPD and prior trauma. Clinical implications of these results and suggested directions for future research are discussed.

A cause for bias may be the relative reluctance of many men to seek support for the emotional distress that is the origin of their urge to self-injure. Many men find themselves within a culture that rewards avoiding seeking support, especially medical support, at all costs. As Wedge explains, "My grandfather did his best to avoid doctors at all costs, no matter how ill he was. I had to think long and hard, for many years, before standing up and demanding support from the NHS." ...

Coping Vs. Suicide

There is a perception that women are better at 'expressing themselves' than men, and that men are often thought of as more comfortable coping with their emotions on their own. Despite the evidence that men suffer emotional stress to the same extent as women, it is still culturally expected that men will remain a 'stiff upper-lip' and keep their emotions 'in control'.

And yet we know for a fact that suicide is one of the highest causes of death for men, especially young men. It is incredibly sad that society places such a great deal of pressure on men to remain 'strong' that some men would rather commit suicide than consider talking about their emotional distress.

Not an Indication of Weakness

Self-injury has nothing to do with either 'weakness' or 'strength', whatever those words might mean. Self-injury is a

Boys Self-Injure Too

Contrary to popular belief, this is not a disorder exclusively seen with adolescent girls; boys self-injure too. However, statistics on the number of boys vs. girls who self-injure are hard to come by. That's because self-injury is often overlooked by clinicians and may be hidden or unreported by patients. Often, not even family and close friends know of the existence or the extent of self-injuring behavior. That may be due to the contradictory nature of the behavior—it's a cry for help, but it's also a source of shame that the teen is compelled to repeat in secret.

"Help Stop Self-Injury," RNWeb.com,
November 2005, http://rnweb.com.

coping mechanism that allows people to deal with their emotional distress, which, of course, cannot be compared from person to person. It is nonsense to say that a person who self-injures is in any way 'weaker' than a person who does not, because their emotional states can't be compared like height, weight, or hair colour.

Self-injury is not about 'strength' or 'weakness', but rather about finding a way to cope with overwhelming negative emotions, stresses, etc. Self-injury is a last-ditch attempt to cope with these factors, when the other options appear to be only an inability to function, or worse, suicide.

It is worth noting that self-injury has the potential to affect all men, regardless of age, race, religion, sexuality, etc. Coming out as gay may well be a stress inducing time but self-injury isn't related to sexuality, and can affect people from all cultures and backgrounds: rugby players, actors, high-powered city executives, teachers, doctors, builders . . . in short, anyone and everyone.

LifeSIGNS believes that although self-injury is a coping mechanism, there are less damaging ways to cope with emotional distress. LifeSIGNS doesn't tell anyone to 'stop' self-injury outright, but we do believe that over time many people can find alternative coping mechanisms and we endeavour to support people as they do so. A person will only be able to move away from self-injuring once they have found a different and more effective way to cope.

Periodical Bibliography

The following articles have been selected to supplement the diverse views presented in this chapter.

Alyson Buck — "Suicide and Self-Harm," *Practice Nurse*, September 10, 2004.

T. Suzanne Eller — "Cutting Edge: Why Even Christian Teens Aren't Immune from the Epidemic of Self-Mutilation," *Today's Christian Woman*, January–February 2005.

Dan Herbeck — "Self-Mutilation by Teens Raises Growing Alarm," *Buffalo News*, April 22, 2007.

Irish Medical News — "Shocking Rise of Teenage Self-Harm Cases," April 5, 2007.

Michelle Malkin — "Youth Cutting Craze Can't Be Ignored," *Grand Rapids Press*, February 24, 2005.

Network World — "Internet Providing Haven for Teens Who Cut, Burn Selves," May 2, 2005.

January W. Payne — "Invitation to Harm: MySpace's Risky Subculture," *The Citizen*, July 7, 2006.

Shana Ross and Nancy Lee Heath — "Two Models of Adolescent Self-Mutilation," *Suicide and Life-Threatening Behavior*, Fall 2003.

Sandy Fertman Ryan — "The Silent Scream," *Girls' Life*, August–September 2005.

Sarah Viren — "Prevalence of 'Cutting' Is Revealed," *Houston Chronicle*, November 13, 2006.

James L. Whitlock, et al. — "The Virtual Cutting Edge: The Internet and Adolescent Self-Injury," *Developmental Psychology*, December 16, 2005.

Alex Williams — "Eating to Harm Myself," *Community Care*, January 27, 2005.

CHAPTER 2

Does Body
Modification Constitute
Self-Mutilation?

Chapter Preface

Self-mutilation has often been defined as the infliction of damage on one's own body as a way to cope with overwhelming feelings or to release emotional pain. Many experts make a distinction between self-injurious behavior and body modification, such as body piercing, tattooing, scarification, and cosmetic surgery. While body modification does inflict injury, immediate physical damage is not the intended effect. According to Armando Favazza, body modification is a socially sanctioned form of self-harm that may be done for the purposes of ritual, spiritual enlightenment, and cultural tradition. Body modification in the western world is often ornamental (in the case of piercings), trendy (in the case of tattooing), or undertaken to improve physical appearance or health (in the case of cosmetic surgery). As such, body modification is commonly understood as a way to boost self-esteem or to express one's individuality. For example, freelance writer Rose Cooper sees her rose tattoo as an emblem of her identity: "It was my rite of passage, my declaration to the world at large, that I had come to accept myself, love myself, and was henceforth going to run my own life."

Yet some analysts draw a connection between body modification and unhealthy forms of self-mutilation. For instance, political science professor Sheila Jeffreys maintains that medical procedures such as breast implant surgery and sex reassignment surgery are forms of self-injurious behavior in which "the cutting is carried out by proxies for a profit." Like teenagers who cut their forearms to find release from emotional pain, many people may have surgery to find release from anguish about their physical appearance or sexuality. As Jeffreys argues, self-mutilation can be a response to "low social status, sexual and physical abuse, or severe emotional distress created by a male dominant society which does not accept women's varied body shapes or condemns homosexuality." In a similar vein, columnist Melanie Phillips contends that body modifications such as piercing and tattooing reflect an increasingly fragmented and violent society: "For this is a culture the inner emptiness of which finds expression in both violence and self-mutilation, to retreat from civilized values, deny reality, and take refuge in a cosmetic defiance and pretence."

In the following chapter, several experts and writers continue this discussion on if and when body modification constitutes self-mutilation.

> *"Some young people who are already self-mutilating in private . . . graduate to the extreme forms of what are now called 'body modification.'"*

Body Modification Is a Form of Self-Mutilation

Sheila Jeffreys

Cutting one's own flesh, body piercing, tattooing, and cosmetic surgery are all forms of self-mutilation which should be opposed, argues Sheila Jeffreys in the following viewpoint. Increasingly, self-harm is perpetrated by surgeons who capitalize on society's rejection of certain body types and its condemnation of homosexuality, she points out. For example, those who are ashamed of their physical features or who believe they are the wrong sex can find professionals to mutilate their bodies for a profit. In addition, self-mutilators sometimes become drawn to more dangerous forms of body modification, such as tongue-splitting and amputation. Jeffreys is an associate professor of political science at the University of Melbourne.

As you read, consider the following questions:

1. What does Jeffreys mean by "self-mutilation by proxy"?

Sheila Jeffreys, "Body Modification as Self-Mutilation by Proxy," *On Line Opinion*, April 10, 2006. Reproduced by permission.

2. What is the origin of breast enlargement, according to the author?

3. How much was the U.S. cosmetic industry worth in the year 2003, according to Jeffreys?

The cutting up that girls do secretly in their bedrooms, the nipple piercing that is performed in high street studios, breast implant surgery, sex reassignment surgery, are connected. They are all forms of self-mutilation, and increasingly the cutting is carried out by proxies for a profit. They are responses to low social status, sexual and physical abuse or severe emotional distress created by a male dominant society which does not accept women's varied body shapes or condemns homosexuality.

Who Self-Mutilates?

Self-mutilation is overwhelmingly the behaviour of girls and young women. Its most common form is cutting of the forearm with razors, or other sharp implements, though other areas of the body can be injured. It is a common behaviour. An estimated two million young women in the US regularly self-mutilate. Girls and women who have no outlet for the rage and pain they experience from male violence and abuse and from the other injuries of a male dominant culture, attack their own bodies.

Often they are emotionally disassociated from their bodies, having learnt this technique to survive abuse. Self-mutilation breaches the barriers they have created and allows them to "feel". The frequency of self-mutilation by young women fits into a context of increasing mental and physical health problems in teenage girls.

Fashionable Forms of Self-Mutilation

I call the practices in which women, and some men, request others to cut up their bodies—as in cosmetic surgery, transsexual surgery, amputee identity disorder (pursuit of limb amputation) and other forms of sadomasochism—self-mutilation by proxy. The proxy, such as the surgeon, the piercer in a piercing studio, the sadist, takes the role that in self-mutilation is more normally taken by the mutilator themselves, and in private. The proxy gains financial benefit, sexual excitement, or both, from carrying out the mutilation.

In the 1990s self-injury perpetrated by proxies became fashionable through the piercing, cutting and tattooing industry. The private self-mutilation born of despair and self-directed rage at abuse and oppression was exploited by piercing entrepreneurs. Piercing studios were set up in cities throughout the western world offering various forms of self-injury to make a profit for the perpetrators.

The forms of injury provided by these studios and independent operators ranged from bellybutton piercings to the extremes of spearing straight through the torso as carried out by the Californian ex-advertising executive Fakir Musafar. The practices stemmed from two main sources, punk fashion and gay male sadomasochism.

Gay male fashion designers placed pierced models on their catwalks, and helped to inscribe a practice that had symbolised gayness, onto the bodies of conventional young women and some young men. The practices were enveloped in new age philosophy, said to be "tribal" in their reflection of the practices of African and other non-western peoples, and carried out by "modern primitives".

The majority of those acquiring piercings and tattooings were simply being fashionable rather than deliberately pursuing pain and the mortification of the flesh. Cutting, piercing and tattooing have quickly become commonplace and socially acceptable among constituencies of young women and gay men, even though they are recent additions to the repertoire of beauty practices. But some young people who are already self-mutilating in private are attracted to more than just mul-

"Ugliness" as Illness

We are surrounded by very clear images and messages that tell us how we should look, and how we most definitely should not look. Women who think that they are suffering from the ills of ugliness (and I believe that a great many do) feel that they can be cured or feel better if they have cosmetic surgery or buy more clothes or make-up—in other words, by consuming. . . .

Everything that is deeply and essentially feminine—life expressed in our faces, the feeling of our skin, the shape of our breasts, the transformations and changes in our skin after childbirth—is being reclassified as ugly and ugliness as an illness. One-third of women's lives are marked by aging, one-third of our bodies are fatty tissues, and both of these have been transformed into surgically-correctable problems. So women can only feel healthy if they are a third of their natural selves.

Anna Arroba, Women's Health Journal, *January–March 2003.*

tiple piercings. They graduate to the extreme forms of what are now called "body modification".

Extreme Body Modification

Internet websites encourage practices such as tongue splitting, suspension from hooks in shoulder muscles, and castration. They show photos with fresh blood and are creating self-harming networks. Male pornophiles can pay to access the photos for the satisfaction of seeing girls being cut up.

One extreme product of this movement is the development of "body integrity identity disorder" (BIID) (previously called amputee identity disorder). Some of the psychiatrists and surgeons who have been involved in the creation of an industry of sex reassignment surgery are now working together to get BIID recognised in the US diagnostic and statistical manual. If they achieve this then in the future they may legally cut off the limbs of those who say that they have always felt uncomfortable with their body shape.

A Scottish surgeon has already cut legs off two healthy men. The Internet is enabling those experimenting with amputating parts of their bodies, such as fingers, and seeking to lose one or more limbs to grow in numbers and support each other's self-harming behaviour.

Health Issues

All of the practices of piercing, tattooing and cutting can cause severe physical harm and even medical emergencies. About 10–15 per cent of piercings get infected. The majority of problems are caused by staphylococcus aureus and streptococcus. Infection with pseudomonas can be dangerous because it can liquify ear cartilage.

Other problems include candidal infections of the navel, and moist areas such as genitalia and the nose. Infections can arise from trauma-induced tears. Some people form keloids or scar tissue and diabetic patients should not have piercings. Piercing has been known to cause a range of other infections including tuberculosis, tetanus, hepatitis, and toxic shock syndrome. The practice of branding hurts a great deal. Tongue piercing can create particular problems such as swallowing or inhaling the stud, the formation of cysts, scarring, damage to nerves and veins, neuromas and damage to teeth. The splitting of tongues can lead to loss of the ability to speak.

Cosmetic Surgery

The most common form of severe self-mutilation by proxy is cosmetic surgery and this practice overwhelmingly affects women. Many of the forms of harm promoted to women by television shows and the advertisements of surgeons derive directly from the pornographication of western culture.

Breast enlargement originated in the prostitution by the western armies of occupation of Japanese women after World War II, who were seen as being the wrong shape for men's excitement. In the West it developed from the so-called sexual revolution in the 1960s in which men's practice of buying women in prostitution was destigmatised. The sex industry expanded swiftly in the US through pornography and stripping and the large breasts the male buyers demanded were created at first by silicone injections which caused even more severe harms to health than implants.

More recently labiaplasty, the removal of women's labia to make their genitals fit the pornographic ideal, has become a profitable area for surgeons. Prostituted women in pornography were the first to have their genitalia modified, and the first in western culture to remove genital hair so that men could stare directly at the exposed genitals. Now, of course, the hair removal, called Brazilian waxing, is practiced in what are called beauty salons.

Other forms of invasive and risky surgery are also becoming much more common. Liposuction, in which fat on the tummy or thighs is liquified and sucked out through a tube, is a temporary solution that some women seek to their failure to live up to the dictates of a male-dominant culture. Silicone is put into lips and cheeks, buttocks (in South America in particular) receive implants, faces are cut up and rearranged.

The routinisation of seriously invasive cosmetic surgery is evident in the discussion forums and message boards that the industry has set up in recent years to gain clients and encourage women to pay for their services. The message boards are sections of the websites of cosmetic surgery clinics and referral services. Women's agonised requests for help or reassurance reveal the damage that is being inflicted. Problems that women discuss include swelling, bruising, pain, numbness, itching, smell, unwanted lumps, dents and constipation.

Risks of Surgery

There are deaths too. Major surgery requires anaesthesia and always involves some risk. Olivia Goldsmith, the US author of the novel on which the movie *First Wives Club* was based, suffered a heart attack from a bad reaction to the anaesthetic during a routine cosmetic surgery procedure to tighten skin on her neck. This unregulated abuse by surgeons who should do no harm does not arouse the outrage that it should because there is a societal acceptance that women should suffer to be beautiful.

The seriously invasive surgery involved in breast implantation, for instance, might be considered savage if it were carried out at a body modification convention. When it is done by surgeons in the name of relieving the supposedly ordinary distress of women about their appearance it can be seen as unremarkable. Also there is huge profit in it. The cosmetic surgery industry in the US was estimated in 2003 to be worth $US8 billion a year.

The practices of mutilation that are being carried out on the bodies of women, girls and vulnerable categories of men in the early 21st Century are savage and increasing in their brutality. Underlying the demand for these practices is the despair of those with low social status, particularly women and gay men. The harms of misogyny, sexual and physical abuse and gay-hating, create the ability of those who self-mutilate to disassociate emotionally from their bodies, and to blame their bodies for their distress.

The cosmetic surgeons, piercers and cutters, sadists, those who watch cutting and SM performances on the Internet or in practice for sexual thrills, and those who create academic careers out of making the cutting up seem glamorous or avant garde, are parasitic on these harms and help to perpetuate them.

> "Numerous people who mark themselves
> . . . celebrate their bodies; their scars,
> they say, are unique artistic expressions
> displayed on their own skin."

Body Modification Is Often a Form of Self-Expression

Kathlyn Gay and Christine Whittington

Body modification—particularly intentional scarring and branding—is increasingly accepted as a ritual practice and as a form of self-expression, write Kathlyn Gay and Christine Whittington in the following viewpoint. Cutting and other kinds of skin marking were widespread among many indigenous peoples, who engaged in scarring for religious purposes, and certain tribal groups still practice scarificaton as a marker of status and as a rite of passage. In addition, many Americans and Europeans have taken up skin marking as a way to identify themselves as members of select groups and to celebrate their uniqueness. Gay and Whittington are the authors of Body Marks: Tattooing, Piercing, and Scarification.

As you read, consider the following questions:

1. What are keloids, according to the authors?
2. What purposes does scarification serve for the people of Benin, according to Gay and Whittington?
3. According to the authors, what does the branding process usually involve?

A scar is defined as "a mark on the body after a surface injury heals," which seems benign enough. After all, countless people show off their "battle scars" while telling elaborate tales about injuries or surgeries. Even a president took part in this type of show-and-tell. When President Lyndon B. Johnson (1963–1969) told reporters about his successful operation to remove his gallbladder, he both shocked and amused the press by picking up his shirt and pointing to his scar.

Yet the word also has a sinister connotation, as was evident in *Scarface*, a classic 1930s gangster film; the gangster's scarred face instantly suggests that he's a menace. A scar can also refer to a trauma—a tragic accident, a death, or other life event that leaves an indelible imprint, or psychological scar, on a person. In addition, the word is a metaphor for environmental destruction—pristine land is often scarred by mining, logging, road and dam building, and other industrial activities.

So what does it mean when someone voluntarily has a scar produced on his or her body? Is this a negative appraisal or proud assessment of self? An attention-getting device? The result of a psychological illness?

What Is Scarification?

Scarification, like extreme body piercing, is frequently associated with counterculture or alternative lifestyles, such as those in SM [sadomasochistic] relationships and the modern primitive movement. But since the late 1980s, scarification has become increasingly popular across the United States and

Canada. It has moved out of the subculture and is practiced in numerous tattoo and body piercing studios. Nevertheless, it's not for the faint-hearted. Why? Because it involves branding—burning the skin, usually with hot metal—or cutting the skin. Both activities can be painful, and after healing both create scars, a process known as cicatrization. The terms scarification and cicatrization are often used interchangeably.

Not all scars are flat on the skin. Some form keloids—excessive growth of fibrous tissues that create a thick scar that rises above the skin surface. Keloids are more likely to form on dark-skinned people than on those with light skin. In some cases, ashes, clay, ink, or other material may be rubbed into a cut to form sharply elevated keloids.

Skin type, whether it's thin or dense, also determines how scars will form. The healing process plays a role as well. Some people remove their scabs and repeat their cuts in order to develop a more visible scar. Because no person's body is exactly like another's, the scar that forms will have its own unique characteristics.

Cutting as a Tribal Practice

For thousands of years people have cut their bodies to produce scars, usually as part of religious or rite-of-passage rituals. Scarring was a widespread practice among the indigenous people of New Zealand and Australia, for example. Maori men of New Zealand covered their faces with tattoo markings that were actually carvings and would be called ink rubbings today. A Maori artist of moko (carving of the face) sketched a design on a man's skin and then used a bone chisel to cut into the skin similar to the way woodcarvings are made. "Ink would be placed in the cuts to create the tattoo. The process could take days or weeks depending on the individual's tolerance for pain."

Scarring was common among the indigenous aborigines of Australia, but it is "now restricted almost entirely to parts of

Arnhem Land. Scarring is like a language inscribed on the body, where each deliberately placed scar tells a story of pain, endurance, identity, status, beauty, courage, sorrow or grief."

A body art exhibit traveling through Australia in 2000 and 2001 explained that a practice of the past required "Wardaman people [to] have two cuts on each shoulder, two on the chest and four on the belly. Jawoyn people only have one cut on the shoulder, one on the chest and a big long one on the belly. Other people have three cuts on the shoulder and many on the belly." The cutting ritual took place when young people turned sixteen or seventeen years of age. Without the scars a person could not take part in ceremonial events, including marriages and burials. A sharp stone made the cuts and burned wood or ash placed on the wound stopped the bleeding and promoted healing.

In Papua New Guinea, it was common to initiate girls at puberty with markings on the abdomen. The first menstrual period was a time for cuttings under the breasts and on the back. After a woman's first child was born, final markings were made on the back, neck, buttocks, arms, and legs.

Scars also show family heritage, membership in a particular community, and social class. . . .

Scarring as Art and Ritual

Among the Yoruba in Nigeria, Africa, body scarification is an art form and ritual based on a proverb that says, "Open your hand, here are lines." The lines provide "visual identification and signify political allegiances or biographical facts regarding a person. Women have the most designs placed onto their bodies. The most common scarification sites are the face, neck, chest, abdomen, back, arms, back of hands, calf or lower leg and thighs."

Scarification is practiced in many other African countries as well. Yombe women of Zaire were marked with crosshatch scars over most of their bodies. This indicated their high sta-

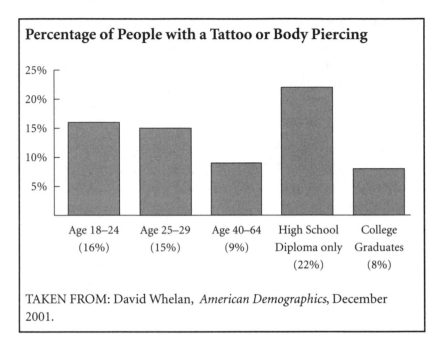

Percentage of People with a Tattoo or Body Piercing

Age 18–24 (16%)	Age 25–29 (15%)	Age 40–64 (9%)	High School Diploma only (22%)	College Graduates (8%)

TAKEN FROM: David Whelan, *American Demographics*, December 2001.

tus and identified their culture. For the Bini, or people of Benin, scarification has served another purpose. According to Bini belief, the process heals or purifies the body. It has also been a way to indicate that girls and boys have become adults. In addition, scarification has symbolized marital commitment. . . .

Among the Luba of central Africa "scarification patterns and their meanings vary from region to region," but some marks impart an enduring message. For example, "Impolo are marks beneath the eyes to add cheerfulness to the smile . . . Nkaka is a pattern of triangles across the chest symbolizing the Luba belief that women contain and guard spiritual knowledge that men, especially Luba officials, must obey." . . .

Scarring as Personal Expression

The scarification practices of indigenous groups in various parts of the world have prompted some Americans and Europeans today to mark their bodies in a similar fashion. While it's not unusual for people to cut themselves to create their scars, the more cautious have sought out artists with cutting expertise. Usually practitioners use a surgical scalpel or laser, cutting into the skin about 1/16 inch (2 mm). They may add tattoo ink, black ash, or other material so a keloid will develop.

What types of designs are created? They vary greatly, ranging from simple parallel lines, such as those used by native people, to intricate designs created by an artist or the person being cut. For example, a cutting design could look like a collar and tie on a man's chest, or the design could be connecting spirals covering a person's entire back.

In the body-art community today, scarification is considered a "natural" way to decorate the skin because it stems from prehistoric times. Although scarification can sometimes be one of the most dangerous forms of skin modification, those who mark their bodies in this manner are taking part in rituals—individual and group rites of passage—that to them have profound meanings and are part of their attempts to demonstrate who they are. This is especially true of those who are branded, which is another form of scarification.

Branding

The practice of branding to create scars certainly is not new. Since ancient times, branding has been a way to show proof of slave and livestock ownership. Criminals and army deserters in many parts of the world were branded as a form of punishment or for identification. In addition, branding has been and still is a rite of passage in many cultures; a brand marks a special life event such as coming of age, a wedding, or a birth.

Branding may also be a ceremonial event, an initiation into a hate group, gang, or an alternative community, for example. Members of music groups sometimes are branded to show their kinship. Branding is also popular on college campuses. Although branding is not sanctioned by Greek fraternity and sorority organizations, the practice has a long tradition among black fraternity brothers. Some have chosen slave designs to symbolize connections with their ancestors. More commonly, brands are fraternity letters. In addition, an increasing number of sorority sisters have taken part in branding rituals.

Among athletes, famous basketball star Michael Jordan has a fraternity brand on his chest. Other professional ballplayers have Omega Psi Phi or Kappa Alpha Psi brands seared on their arms, calves, thighs, or backsides.

The Branding Process

How is a person branded? In some cases, people brand themselves or have friends do the job, although this is not recommended by professional branding artists. On occasion, amateurs experiment with dry ice, which burns the skin. For the most part, though, amateurs use whatever metal objects happen to be at hand and can be shaped into designs—paper clips, coat hangers, needles, cans, or screws. Horseshoes are common branding tools among fraternities, according to the Texas Tech Health Sciences Center.

Several years ago, a *Washington Post* reporter described a branding ritual that took place at Howard University:

> Imagine a carefully fashioned coat hanger, slow-roasted over blue-green flame of a Magic Chef range, heading for the fleshy expanse of your upper arm, your chest or the side of your behind. For a fraction of a second, you can feel the heat before it touches your skin. Your heart races and instinctively you want to draw back. But you don't. Because you want your brand to be sweet. Or if you think you'll move, you brace yourself, holding onto a sink or table; or perhaps you get somebody else to hold you down.
>
> Then comes the "hit," a quick "Psssssssst." Or maybe it's a "crackle" or "pop," not unlike the sound of Rice Krispies

soaking in a bowl of milk. They say it doesn't really hurt. But the smell of burning flesh can be weird. Especially when it's yours.

In a commercial studio, the process usually begins with a small bar of surgical steel that is heated until it is glowing orange, 1100°F (593°C). In some cases, a branding artist uses silver objects, ceramic pieces, or metal items like bolts and screws to create scar designs. A cautery pen, usually used for medical purposes such as removing abnormal skin tissue, is also used for branding, especially when designs are intricate or placed on a sensitive part of the body.

Whatever the branding implement, it is pressed onto a person's arm, back, shoulder, buttocks, thigh, ankle, or other part of the body, producing a third-degree burn. Each hit of hot metal, called a strike, must be precise and held on the skin for only one or two seconds. The strike is accompanied by a small puff of smoke and the smell of burning flesh. For a second there could be searing pain, but the nerves are destroyed so the pain does not last. In fact, some people who are branded say that the pain causes an "endorphin rush"—that is, the brain is numbed for a time, rather like the effects of an anesthetic or powerful pain reliever. . . .

Body Art or Self-Injury?

In spite of the constant warnings that branding or cutting oneself is a dangerous form of body marking, countless individuals who practice scarification produce their own brands or cuts. Warnings seldom discourage a person intent on self-scarification, especially by cutting. In the view of Professor Myrna Armstrong of Texas Tech Medical Sciences Center, cutting patterns in the skin to create a scar "borders on self-mutilation." In other words, people want to hurt themselves because it is their way of releasing psychological or emotional pain.

Indeed it is sometimes difficult to determine whether people who cut themselves are doing so because they want to create scar designs or because they are addicted to self-injury, or self-inflicted violence (SIV), a serious psychological problem. An estimated two to three million Americans engage in SIV. They carry psychological scars sometimes because they have been physically or sexually abused. Cutting, they say, relieves or dulls emotional pain, distress, frustration, or other negative feelings. After a cutting they frequently express a great sense of relief seeing the blood running down an arm, leg, or other part of the body. People who need help with self-injury problems can find information and advice on various Web sites. One of the sites that contains links to numerous resources is www.smalltime.com/notvictims/cutting.html.

Yet that does not mean all people who cut themselves to produce scars suffer a psychological disorder. In spite of the stigma attached to self-cuttings, numerous people who mark themselves in this manner are proud of their scarifications. Some contend that the process brings a level of awareness beyond anything imaginable. In this manner, they celebrate their bodies; their scars, they say, are unique artistic expressions displayed on their own skin.

> "[Through] the bold symbolism of body-art ... [tribes] hold onto a fierce determination to maintain their cultural identity."

Body Modification Is Often a Marker of Cultural Identity

Debbie Jefkin-Elnekave

In tribal regions of Africa and Asia, piercings, tattoos, and self-inflicted scars are an indicator of cultural identity, explains Debbie Jefkin-Elnekave in the following viewpoint. Adornments and skin markings are often a way to define status, to celebrate beauty, to exhibit bravery, or to appease spirits, she points out. Moreover, body modification provides a way to distinguish tribal members from people who are part of the surrounding society, thus ensuring a strong group identity. Jefkin-Elnekave is a photographer, travel writer, and tour leader.

As you read, consider the following questions:

1. Why do Hamer men notch their ears, according to the author?

Debbie Jefkin-Elnekave, "Tribal Identity Through Body Art," *Skipping Stones*, vol. 16, no. 1, January–February 2004, pp. 34–35. Copyright 2004 Skipping Stones. Reproduced by permission.

2. In Jefkin-Elnekave's view, what are the possible origins of the neck-stretching practices among the PaDuang women of Thailand?

3. What is the purpose of the geometric tattoos on the hands of the Dongariya Kondh women, according to the author?

Members of the Longia Saora tribe, in Orissa, Eastern India, stretch their ear lobes by placing increasingly larger balsa wood earplugs into their pierced ears. After several months, the earlobe is so elastic that it nearly reaches the shoulders.

Why do people adorn, tattoo, scarify or pierce their bodies? This question had never occurred to me until I traveled throughout tribal Africa and Asia. Of all the ways that a culture distinguishes itself—through architecture, religion, ceremonies—ritual decoration is the most fascinating of all. At first glance, each tribe or ethnic group is captivating for its own unique appearance. But, for all their differences, many of their reasons for adorning, tattooing, or piercing their bodies are the same: to convey beauty, wealth, status, bravery or even to appease the spirits.

The Beauty of Accessorizing

The remote parts of Orissa, Eastern India, provide a perfect environment for the preservation of several tribal groups. The women of Bonda tribe (who live not too far from the Longia Saora tribe) are known for their colorful costumes. They artfully cover themselves with hundreds of strands of yellow, orange and white beads, which cascade elegantly like a brilliant bib. The crowning accessories include a beaded skullcap over a shaven head, silver necklace and earrings, and a brass nose ring.

The men of the elusive Dani tribe of Irian Jaya are immediately distinguished by their dress, or lack thereof. They wear

Tattooing in Samoa

In old-time Samoa, the majority of women were not tattooed. The male tattoo, however, was obligatory, as it marked the transition from boyhood to manhood. "The woman must bear children. The man must be tattooed," says one tattooing song. Both sexes must endure pain—the woman through the laws of nature and the man through those of his culture.

Tattooing is certainly a longer, and therefore more painful, process for Samoan men to endure. While the women only have their thighs tattooed, the men are tattooed from the knees to slightly above the waistline in front and on the back; only the skin of the private parts is left unmarked. And while the female tattoo consists of thin lines, the male tattoo features large areas that are completely filled in with black dye.

Anders Ryman, World and I, *June 2004.*

only a privacy gourd for modesty. The Dani are well-attuned to the resources of their land, which provides them with superb accessories, such as white lime, flowers, fur, shells, feathers and curved bone nosepieces.

Courtship and Marriage

Hamer women of Ethiopia beautify their bodies with elaborate decorations and scars. They apply a concoction of red ochre and animal grease to their hair and style it according to their marital status. If a woman is married, she wears two iron torque necklaces, called essentes, or three if she is her husband's first wife. An engaged woman wears a leather band around her neck, signifying that her fiance has completed the bullah, or "jumping of the bulls", a rite that testifies to his manhood and his right to marry. A young girl of marriageable age wears a metal visor called a balle to indicate her status. This symbol of eligibility simplifies things at the weekly market, which is a common meeting place for young men and women. A Hamer man notches his ear on the occasion of his first marriage, and the edges of his ears are pierced once for each wife he has.

In the Wodaabes of West Africa, the most dramatic beauty custom is the gerewol courting ritual. Young men adorn themselves with extravagant costumes and makeup, carefully applied to highlight their cherished elements of beauty: sinewy bodies, thin noses and lips, and white eyeballs and teeth. Once festooned in full gerewol regalia, the men hold hands, form a circle or line and start to chant and sway. The young girls choose the most handsome men, and many of these pairings result in marriage.

Wealth and Status

Wealth is measured differently from one tribe to another, but one thing is consistent: if they've got it, they flaunt it.

Cowry shells are a measure of wealth in the Dani tribe, although these highlanders may not have seen the sea! The tribe's chiefs and most affluent members wear a breastplate made up of the shells to display wealth. The value of a shell is determined by its size, shape, color, ribbing and luster. The most valuable are the smaller shells with the convex back removed. Top-grade shells are given names and accompanied by a detailed history of every transaction in which they were involved. The shells take years to travel from the coastal region to the highlands, passing through many hands en route.

PaDaung women of Thailand are known for the practice of stretching their necks. The number and value of the rings confers status on the wearer's family. Girls are first fitted with the rings at the age of five or six, on a day prescribed by the horoscopic findings of the village shaman. A new ring is added to the stack each year until marriage. There are several theories about the origin of this practice. Some say that it rendered the women incapable of farming or heavy labor, thereby protecting them against kidnapping by invading tribes and slave traders. Others believe it prevented tiger bites. Yet another explanation is that it is purely an expression of feminine beauty.

Intimidation and Bravery

Dani men are notorious for battles over pigs, women and land-rights. The warriors set forth for battle naked, but covered with a mixture of ashes and pig grease. This is meant to intimidate their adversaries by appearing so fierce that they paralyze the enemy with fear.

The Bume of Ethiopia are warriors who fight over grazing land, and their body scarification is closely related to their warfare. They are earned after a hunt or kill, and given in a complex ritual. These prestigious marks are a record of personal achievement.

Across the Omo River from the Bume, Hamer men wear their hair in a multi-colored, painted clay bun. It is a symbol of bravery and courage.

Appeasing the Spirits

Akha women of Thailand wear an elaborate silver headdress that might weigh as much as ten pounds, yet they wear it all the time: to festivals, to labor in the fields, even to bed. The point of these ornate adornments? Quite simply, as strict animists who practice spirit worship, they believe it would offend the spirits if they did not wear their finery.

The most distinguishing feature of Orissa's Dongariya Kondh women is the geometric tattoos on their hands. As animists, they believe that when they die and turn into spirits, these markings will help them recognize each other in the spirit world.

Living in the Remnants of Time

Beyond the significant and bold symbolism of body-art, jewelry, clothing and hairstyles, there is another, more timeless reason for why tribes create a visual uniformity that so obviously sets them apart: They hold onto a fierce determination to maintain their cultural identity. This visual uniformity helps keep them together and also keeps everyone else out. The more rituals a tribe binds into its culture, the less likely that members of the group will assimilate into the surrounding society.

Some of these tribal groups have recently experienced their first contact with the outside world, while others have survived years of exploitation, repression or modernization. It is my hope that they will not be "civilized" into extinction.

By remaining true to tribal identity, they maintain a perpetual memorial to their ancestors. These rituals honor the past, nurture the future, and preserve extraordinary people living in the remnants of time.

"Body mutilation is the decoration of choice for an age which has turned violence into a modish cult."

Body Modification Is a Sign of Cultural Depravity

Melanie Phillips

In the following viewpoint, British columnist and author Melanie Phillips decries the trendiness of body modifications such as tattooing, piercing, and cosmetic surgery. She equates these fashion statements with self-mutilation and sees their popularity as a sign of a morally corrupt, shallow, and spiritually empty culture. Moreover, she asserts, body modification reflects low self-esteem and a hatred of the body rooted in a desire to evade reality.

As you read, consider the following questions:

1. What do Botox injections do, according to Phillips?

2. In what ways do tattoos expose a "hollowness of character," according to the author?

3. What is self-mutilation an outward sign of, in Phillips' opinion?

There was a time when sentimentality meant wearing your heart on your sleeve. Now it's more likely to be carved into the nape of your neck.

[English professional footballer] David Beckham has revealed a startling tattoo below his hair line depicting a green cross with wings extending almost from ear to ear. This enigmatic example of neck art has occasioned wonderment and disgust in equal measure.

At the same time, the quiz show host Anne Robinson has come clean about her recent face-lift, which she had done because she didn't want a 'face like a road map'. Now, there's nothing like the boast of yet another celebrity about having her face lifted to cause the faces of everyone else to fall. But surely, something more than mere vanity is at work here.

A Fortune on Blemishes?

After all, isn't it somewhat strange that while people like Anne Robinson spend a fortune having blemishes removed from their physiognomy, people like David Beckham are busy putting fresh ones indelibly on?

The Beckham winged cross has hardly enhanced its owner's natural beauty. It is, in short, thuggish and repellent. It is also very large, permanent and, since it is so visible on the back of his neck, in your face (so to speak). Even the tattooist expressed concern about using such a prominent location.

So what does its appearance mean? Amateur psychologists speculate it is some kind of tough-guy statement to counter the recent torrid allegations about the state of his marriage.

But this is the ninth tattoo to adorn the Beckham torso. Others sport his wife's name spelled out in Hindi, his son's name in inch-high Gothic lettering, his iconic shirt number 7, and a Michelangelo angel on his right arm.

Revulsion at the Bookstore

There is an employee at my local bookstore. The first time he waited on me I went weak in the knees, and not because he looks like Johnny Depp. He had a ring. In his nose. Toro style. It was big enough to hold one of my dinner napkins. . .

Does anybody else suffer frissons of revulsion, or is it just me? I cannot let him wait on me. I like chatting with wait staff and servers as much as the next patron. But if I can't look someone in the face because of his piercings, please take my place in line. I'll await the next cashier.

Debra Darvick, Newsweek, *July 12, 2004.*

Designer Wounds

This goes beyond one silly footballer dreaming up new ways to make himelf the centre of attention. For what was once the adornment of choice for sailors or skinheads has now become high fashion—particularly for women, who sport tattoos on their shoulders or in more discreet places.

Such tattoos are considered sexy. But however feminine the design, they display the innate ugliness of any disfigurement. They are not so much body art as designer wounds.

They are akin to the other fashion for using skin as decoration through body piercing. So people sport studs in tongues, diamonds through navels, and barbells, spikes and rings hung with bells and whistles.

Cosmetic surgery, too, is a bodily assault course. Botox injections to smooth out wrinkles employ a poison which, if used long enough, makes the facial muscles atrophy from lack of use. In addition to having their thighs and stomachs sucked out and their breasts pumped up, women are even having their toes shortened so their feet can fit into fashionable shoes. And they queue for collagen injections to plump up their lips, which instead of turning them into sex kittens make them resemble instead the inhabitants of a goldfish bowl.

This Cinderella illusion seems to have turned the beauty salon into a makeover of the macabre straight out of a horror film. Anne Robinson describes a previous treatment she underwent called 'face lasering', by inviting us to 'imagine the M40 and several layers of tired, worn Tarmac being removed'. For heaven's sake, this was her face, not a three-lane motorway!

Self-Mutilation as Fashion

So what lies behind this bizarre fashion for self-mutilation? Above all, tattooing and body-piercing turn the anti-social into a fashion statement. In these morally topsy-turvy times, it has become the fashion to celebrate or ape the degraded elements of our culture. Hence the foul language, binge drinking, drug taking and sexual debauchery.

Tattooing was always considered to be associated with thuggery, and indeed many men in prison are tattooed. Now, however, as our society slides deeper into the moral mire we have thug chic—or in the case of tattooed women, thug chicks.

By appropriating a symbol of male savagery and feminising it, tattooed women in particular signal a potent breach of a taboo and therefore—to those turned on by such things—a promise that female decorum is merely a veneer concealing a more primitive instinct.

This is all part of a culture which has made a fetish of challenging the very notion of what is disapproved of or even forbidden. There was a time when the deliberate infliction of harm on oneself or on others was illegal. Extreme notions of freedom of choice, however, then turned the infliction of suffering into a right, provided it was 'consensual'.

So what was once considered grievous bodily harm has now become the last word in cool. Body mutilation is the decoration of choice for an age which has turned violence into a modish cult, from sadomasochism clubs to the film *Fight Club* and real-life staged battles between rival gangs of football hooligans.

Hollowness of Character

Tattoos expose a terrible hollowness of character. Their owners appear to believe that displaying feelings makes them real. But in a society where actual feelings are becoming increasingly shallow, committed and faithful relationships are disappearing and emotion is giving way to sentimentality, so it is becoming more important to announce that your emotions are permanent, if only in ink.

Tattoos also reflect a distressing inarticulacy and sense of personal insignificance. Those who wear them think they help them stand out as individuals. In fact, since they reduce individuality to crude slogans or cartoon images, they simply point up the owner's fragile sense of identity.

Above all, tattooing, body piercing and cosmetic surgery all reflect rock-bottom self-esteem. All these procedures mean treating the body with contempt and even hatred in an attempt to deny or evade painful realities.

Face-lifts and other cosmetic surgery are designed to conceal what women have actually become through the effects of aging. They carve out a lie, a fantasy of perfection. They erase experience of life and produce faces which therefore look disturbingly blank and more than a little spooky.

If such surgery denies the progress of the human body, tattoing surely symbolises a denial of the progress of society. For tattooing belongs to ancient cultures where it expressed superstitions, appeased primitive gods or denoted social status.

An Age of Spiritual Emptiness

Beckham thinks his angel tattoos give protection to his wife and children. Such a retreat to primitive ideas fits with the prevailing fashion for scorning the restraints of civilisation. For tattoos are only considered spiritual by people who go in for cults, witchcraft, crystals and other pagan throw-backs which denote what is often smugly referred to as our post-religious age.

In fact, this is an age of spiritual emptiness. The fashion for bodily mutilation is the outward sign of the horrifying increase in those whose sense of themselves is fragile or shattered, very often because of the fragmentation of the family.

It is no surprise that a footballing icon is increasingly disfiguring his splendid physique. Tattooing is a form of wanton damage. One might say that in Beckham's self-mutilation, the hooliganism of the terraces is expressing itself in the vandalism of the body worshipped by the terraces.

For this is a culture the inner emptiness of which finds expression in both violence and self-mutilation, to retreat from civilised values, deny reality and take refuge in a cosmetic defiance and pretence.

> *"Though they may seem a cool means of self-expression, piercings also come with potential dangers."*

Piercing and Tattooing Can Be Dangerous

Pippa Wysong

Body piercings and tattoos have potentially harmful effects, asserts Pippa Wysong in the following viewpoint. Infections and allergies to metals or inks can occur—especially if unsterilized equipment is used in the process—and severe reactions can even lead to death, she points out. The author cautions teens to seriously consider the health risks of these procedures and to seek out licensed professionals if they decide to get pierced or tattooed. Wysong is a freelance journalist specializing in medicine and children's issues.

As you read, consider the following questions:

1. What percentage of teenagers have piercings, according to Wysong?
2. What communicable diseases can be spread through the piercing process, according to the author?

Pippa Wysong, "Modified: Are Piercings and Tattoos Safe?" *Current Health 2: A Weekly Reader Publication*, vol. 32, no. 7, March 2006, pp. 26–30. Copyright 2006 Weekly Reader Corp. Reproduced by permission.

3. In Wysong's words, how do dermatologists get rid of unwanted tattoos?

Alexis Valentino was only 18 months old when her ears were first pierced, a common practice in her Italian family. Now the 16-year-old from West Chester, Pa., has three earrings in each ear plus a belly button ring, and she is likely to have more piercings in her future. Maybe even a tattoo or two.

These days, piercings often go well beyond earlobes. Belly buttons, tongues, ear cartilage, eyebrows, nipples, lips, and even genitals are targets for metallic barbells, delicate chains, and stud jewelry. Tattoos run the gamut of images, from a discreet star to Celtic-inspired bracelets around an arm to huge artistic undertakings with the body as a canvas.

Body art (also called body modification) used to be just for Goths, bikers, and certain cultures both ancient and modern. Today, piercings and tattoos (including decals, henna, or permanent ink) are common. An estimated 23 percent of teens have piercings, about 8 percent have tattoos, and another 21 percent want tattoos. It's all part of the effort to be cool or to do something that looks a little different.

Teens Tell All

At age 12, Alexis opted for second holes in her earlobes, and at 13 she had the third ones put in. When she turned 15, she got her belly button pierced. Does she want more? You bet. "I want to get my tongue pierced," she says.

But her mom put a hold on that, as well as the flower tattoo Alexis would like on her back. In most states, minors need a parent's permission to get a tattoo or a piercing. In some states, it is illegal for minors to get these procedures at all. (The Association of Professional Piercers notes that many regulations exclude piercing done with piercing guns, frequently used at mall kiosks to insert earlobe earrings.)

Alexis's classmate Jessica Adamiak, 15, has pierced ears but is waiting for her parents' OK to get her nose pierced. "My dad keeps saying he wants me to wait until I'm 30. Can you believe that?" she asks.

Problems with Piercings

Though they may seem a cool means of self-expression, piercings also come with potential dangers, cautions Dr. Lynn McKinley-Grant, a dermatologist from Chew Chase, Md. Some problems include

- chipped or cracked teeth caused by chomping on a tongue stud;

- allergic reactions to metals used in jewelry—a severe allergy can even lead to death;

- choking if a tongue ring becomes loose;

- infection, which can cause swelling, pain, and oozing pus, and require a trip to the hospital.

Tongue infections are among the worst to treat, especially when the tongue is so swollen that the stud has to be surgically removed, McKinley-Grant says. The biggest risks for infections are new piercings or trauma to the newly pierced area, such as scratches or bruises. Infections can happen if piercing equipment is not properly sterilized or if a piercing is not cared for properly before it has healed.

Alexis is familiar with the risks after seeing what her older sister Amanda went through. Amanda, 20, has piercings in her earlobe, ear cartilage, nose, and lip. She also has a tattoo she designed herself. Amanda's first problem was a keloid, a big reddish-brown bump that grew at a piercing site on her ear cartilage. Keloids happen when too much scar tissue forms, and they can be quite unsightly. Amanda had to have plastic surgery to remove it.

Preventing the Spread of Diseases During Piercing

The best way to prevent the spread of ... communicable diseases during body piercing is proper needle disposal after use and use of a new needle for each client. Piercing guns are not recommended due to damage to the tissues caused by the pressure of the injection and because they are difficult to resterilize after use. The risk of infection is increased when adolescents attempt to pierce themselves and/or their peers without properly sterilizing the equipment. Teens should be educated about the risk of disease transmission and should be strongly discouraged from performing self-piercing.

Theresa E. Bunger and Betsy M. McDowell,
Journal for Specialists in Pediatric Nursing, *April–June 2004.*

Problems are common in cartilage, according to McKinley-Grant. "It has little blood flow and does not heal as easily as the earlobes," she says. Other big risks from piercings include infection with human immunodeficiency virus (HIV) or hepatitis from reused or unsterilized needles.

Amanda also had problems with a piercing in the flesh between her thumb and forefinger. A severe infection landed her in the emergency room to have the stud removed. But Amanda's problems don't faze Alexis, who plans to get more piercings. Alexis's mom, though cool with the idea of piercing (she has two earrings in each ear herself), is keeping a watchful eye.

Thinking Before Inking

Then there is the allure of tattoos. Although many teens go for temporary ones from decals or henna, others pick the permanent type. It's important to remember that ink tattoos don't go away, says Barbara Freyenberger, a nurse-practitioner at the Children's Hospital of Iowa.

In fact, it's tough to get rid of tattoos if you don't like the pattern anymore or the artwork isn't what you expected. One study showed that close to 4 percent of college students with tattoos had them removed. As people age, tattoo removal is more common.

Over several visits, a dermatologist zaps unwanted tattoos with special medical lasers—a different laser for each color, and each color requires a separate trip. Tattoo removal generally means about $500 to $1,000 per treatment. (And health insurance usually doesn't cover it!) Removal can leave a slight scar and some skin discoloration. "It can take a minimum of eight treatments to completely remove a tattoo," says McKinley-Grant. Some parts of the body scar more than others from the procedure, the worst being the back, chest, and upper arms.

Another hidden danger of tattoos is a lack of regulation in the pigments used in ink. They can vary in quality, and some colors might contain lead, which can cause brain and nerve damage. Some people have allergic reactions to hennas or ink ingredients and can develop a rash or other health problems from the chemicals. In addition, tattoo needles—like piercing instruments—can pass on infections from other clients.

If you decide to get a tattoo, take your time thinking about it, Freyenberger advises. Get it done by a professional in a clean, sanitary environment. Make sure the tattoo artist uses new needles fresh out of the package and that the needles are dipped in fresh (not used) ink pots.

Safety Tips for Piercings and Tattoos

Though tattoos and piercings may look cool, you should seriously mull over the health risks. And consider whether you'll still want the tattoo or piercing when you're in your 20s or 30s—or older. If you decide to go ahead, check the age-limit laws in your state, get your parents' permission, research the medical implications, and find the cleanest, safest shop around.

- Go only to a professional, licensed piercer or tattooist.

- Ask about cleanliness and infection control; if you don't feel safe or get satisfactory answers, leave.

- Only patronize shops that use an autoclave, a device that sterilizes equipment, between customers.

- Make sure the tattooist or piercer uses new needles out of fresh, new packages, and that he or she disposes of needles in a special biohazard container after use.

- Only use a tattooist who throws out leftover ink instead of pouring it back into the bottle.

- For new piercings, wear only noncorrosive metals (stainless steel, 14-karat gold) until the wound has healed.

- Keep the tattoo or piercing clean; don't mess with it until the wounds are healed.

- Remember: Waiting is always an option. If you do decide to get a body piercing or tattoo, consider selecting a discreet place for it on your body. You may not like it later—and if you have it removed, there will be scarring.

> "How different is going under the knife
> in search of youth and beauty from
> some ritual and hidden adolescent cut-
> ting?"

Cosmetic Surgery Can Be a Form of Self-Mutilation

Virginia L. Blum

*In the following viewpoint, Virginia L. Blum argues that cos-
metic surgery is sometimes a form of self-mutilation. Women
who want to make themselves more physically attractive through
cosmetic surgery can become addicted to it, constantly seeking
love and acceptance by sacrificing what they find ugly or shameful about themselves to the surgeon's knife. Like teenagers who
cut themselves to find release from emotional pain, women may
have surgery to relieve themselves of anguish about their appearance, Blum points out. Blum is the author of* Flesh Wounds:
The Culture of Cosmetic Surgery.

As you read, consider the following questions:

1. Why did the actress Farrah Fawcett have cosmetic surgery, according to the author?

Virginia L. Blum, *Flesh Wounds: The Culture of Cosmetic Surgery*. Berkeley: University of California Press, 2003, pp. 268–170, 287–90. Copyright © 2003 by The Regents
of the University of California. Reproduced by permission.

2. What were the circumstances surrounding "Barbara's" addiction to surgery, in Blum's opinion?

3. According to Andrew Morton, quoted by the author, what famous woman was a self-cutter?

"Look at Farrah Now" urges the headline of the 4 July 2000 issue of the *National Enquirer*. I look at Farrah's face and don't recognize her. In her place I see a generic post-op woman, plumped up lips, cheek implants, one eyelid hiked a bit too high, profile with a particular surgical lilt to the tip of the nose. Nothing like Farrah. The article explains that eight years ago Farrah "had work to smooth wrinkles and sun damage." Later, after the breakup of a relationship, claims the *Enquirer*, she had a brow-lift. Subsequent to her performance as Robert Duvall's wife in the film *The Apostle*, she received many "offers of work." "And she was convinced plastic surgery was responsible." So why not even more? "When Farrah landed the role in 'Dr. T and the Women,' as Richard Gere's wife, 'the last thing she wanted was to look old and tired in her close-ups. So, she had a major overhaul,' added the insider." True or not, this is the story of surgical addiction—and why, once you believe that surgery "works," you will keep doing it.

Farrah supposedly needed more surgery to play Gere's wife. It's not just actresses playing the role of the wife who have surgery to keep their faces in check for the hellish close-up. It's also wives who desperately take arms against their faces and bodies to keep their husbands "interested." It's not just actresses who struggle to hold the camera's affection. It's also ordinary women (so many of us) who think that what makes us worthwhile, worth anything, is a pleasing physical appearance. Joyce D. Nash, a psychologist, recounts what she terms a case of surgery addiction:

> Often the surgery addict feels she is fighting a war of attrition with her looks. This was the case for "Barbara." Al-

though Barbara claimed her age was 48, she was actually 54. Despite her blonde hair, endless array of skin creams, and frequent shopping trips for new clothes, Barbara was having difficulty holding her marriage together. Her husband (age 55) was a wealthy businessman who traveled around the world and had casual affairs whenever he could. . . . Barbara had had her face lifted twice in attempts to remain youthful, and while these interventions were technically successful, they never altered her worried and guilty manner. She was very attached to her plastic surgeon, always bringing flowers for his secretary and returning regularly to have the state of her face checked by him.

Nash, who herself had a face-lift, is here trying to distinguish between a normal concern with keeping up one's appearance and the desperate plight of poor Barbara, who blames her aging body for her bad marriage. But Barbara has imbibed thoroughly the cultural lesson about the necessity for women to look good. If her life isn't better, then that must mean she needs another face-lift. Comparing Barbara's story with Farrah's, we have here two different but related plastic surgery addiction narratives: Farrah's is the race against time. In one less than vigilant moment, all might be lost. Barbara, on the other hand, thinks she might have a happy life if she could just get it right this time. If this straying husband was faithful early on in the marriage, then it must be that she is no longer the same. She will go to her plastic surgeon and place her face in his competent hands. He will take care of her—even if her husband won't. Why is Barbara doing this? we might ask. Doesn't she realize that no amount of surgery will transform a chronically unfaithful husband into the picture of fidelity? But she has found another man now, her surgeon, who will restore to her these lost treasures. Losing the love of the camera might feel no different from losing the love of the husband. This is where the surgeon comes in—to rescue the fair princess, unlock the crone body in which she's trapped, release her to her real and happy life. She takes her

Plastic Surgery Addiction

Plastic surgery addiction often stems from a condition called body dysmorphic disorder. This is a disorder that causes a person to consider themselves hideous, no matter how attractive they really are. They feel that if they are not happy, then they must not be beautiful and in order to be happy, they must become beautiful. The problem is that the lack of happiness does not stem from their physical appearance. Once people with this condition turn to plastic surgery, they have to go back for more, because the change in their appearance does not bring the desired effect on their happiness.

Michael Russell, "Plastic Surgery Addiction: Is it Dangerous?"
http://EzineArticles.com.

bow. She is loved once again. Waves of love wash over her, just as Eve Harrington imagines.

It would be hard not to become addicted. It would be hard to stop once you found out it worked. It would be equally hard to stop if you believe it should work and you just haven't yet found the right formula, surgeon, procedure. Whether it's for reconstructive or purely aesthetic reasons, the ongoing sense of imperfection pushes us forward. . . .

They are called delicate self-cutters, most often adolescent females who cut their skin in moments of intolerable anxiety. They make shallow rifts across the surface of their skin. "The cuts are carefully wrought, sometimes simple parallel lines but also intricate patterns; rectangles, circles, initials, even flower-like shapes." These cuts can be a work of art, elevating the body from what is felt to be its abject changes (menstruation, for example) and longings; they can reassert the distinction between the inside and the outside. At the same time, the cuts can function as counterphobic responses to a sense of internal mutilation. The delicate self-cutter becomes herself the agent of a mutilation she dreads passively experiencing. Psychoanalyst Louise Kaplan observes that "a perversion, when it is successful, also preserves the social order, its institutions, the structures of family life, the mind itself from despair and fragmentation." Like many who undergo cosmetic surgery, Kaplan's perverts experience a deep-seated shame that needs correcting and feel defiant rather than guilty about their perversion, which they nevertheless take to be a violation of the moral order.

The surgical patient's shame is intolerable, the thing that drives her or him to the doctor—aging or ugliness or just not being quite beautiful enough. Just outside the operating room, a surgeon explained to me that the patient inside was the "ugly duckling" of her voluptuous family. She was now in the middle of divorce and wanted to improve her appearance. Who can imagine her shame? How can I express the shame I felt for her as her surgeon pronounced the shameful "truth" of her unloveable body.

The genetically blessed, hypertoned, strategically lit bodies of actresses can induce shame in the woman with an ordinary flesh-and-blood body. But even the "real" actress's incapacity to maintain such a body is humorously treated in Mike Nichols's film *Postcards from the Edge*. Actress Suzanne overhears the head of wardrobe complaining to the director about the difficulties of tailoring clothing for the actress's out-of-shape body. They can't put her in shorts because the top of her thighs are shockingly "bulbous." They can't film her on her back during the love scene because her breasts are "out of shape" and will no doubt "disappear under her armpits." They express regret that they hadn't managed to cast in her place another actress whose body was supposed to be "perfect." Many of the women I know, not actresses, just ordinary women, worry about being seen in public in bikinis or short-sleeved tops or shorts rising much beyond the knee, clothes that would disclose to all a shameful and secret part that we keep hidden from view—our flabby thighs, our postpartum middles, our middle-aged arms. Said one surgeon: "I know of many women whose husbands have never seen them nude. I know of women who never go to doctors because they don't want to be seen by them." So, finally they offer themselves up to the surgeon for aesthetic body work, and they are transformed. They can be seen, held, admired. Little by little, we are all becoming movie stars—internally framed by a camera eye.

"The little mutilations take up her mind and enable her to temporarily escape the frightening implications of being transformed physically and emotionally into a woman with the sexual and moral responsibilities of adulthood." Kaplan is writing as though the transition is just one, from girlhood to womanhood, which, for the delicate self-cutter, proves intolerable. What if we were to rethink this universal transition (puberty to womanhood) through the terms of the twenty-first century, where we find the chronological body supplanted by a two-dimensional prototype that is an impossible combination of fashion-centric transitions and age-defying stasis? This is a body always in flux. It can't land on the other side. It can't become and stay comfortably a woman, because it's so difficult and there are always new challenges to face as well as perils to ward off.

Princess Diana was a self-cutter, or so claims biographer Andrew Morton. "On one occasion she threw herself against a glass cabinet at Kensington Palace, while on another she slashed at her wrists with a razor blade. Another time she cut herself with the serrated edge of a lemon slicer; on yet another occasion during a heated argument with Prince Charles, she picked up a penknife lying on his dressing table and cut her chest and her thighs." Reminiscent of Elizabeth Taylor, Diana was a celebrity who seemed literally to embody the shift from flesh to image and back again. Her confessed eating disorder made her beautiful image seem more available, closer up, or rather heightened the exciting tension between flesh and image.

And so how different is going under the knife in search of youth and beauty from some ritual and hidden adolescent cutting? Just because the culture has normalized our pathology (of course, it's thoroughly normal to want to look rested and vigorous enough to compete in the youth-centered workplace), it doesn't mean that cosmetic surgery isn't like any other practice that has us offering up our bodies to the psychical intensities that angrily grip us. Ballerina Gelsey Kirkland describes the experience of her initial round of cosmetic surgeries: "The operations found me laid out on a table, yielding to the touch of their probing fingers. I watched my life through the eyes of their needle, penetrating my heart as well as the outer layers of my skin. I would become hooked on the pain, addicted to the voluptuous misery that bound my sexual identity to ballet, to an ever-increasing threshold of anguish." On the operating table, face up, waiting for hands to crawl inside and tug out the ugliness that is like entrails that eventually regenerate and need to be taken out yet again. We struggle up from intolerable bodies vanquished in the exquisite moment of surgical battle in the theater of operations. I recall the scene of a face-lift. One minute she was lying in the swamp of her aging and flaccid skin, and then slowly her face rose from the chaos, sleek, tautened—as though taking shape out of some primal sea—the shards of her outgrown and useless flesh left behind, spirited away by the surgeon's magic.

You will look in the mirror, smile back at the image reclaimed, and relish the grace period between this operation and the next one. The beast-flesh will grow back.

| *"Cosmetic surgery is a valuable, low-risk investment in your future health, happiness, and well-being."*

Cosmetic Surgery Boosts Self-Esteem

Michelle Copeland

Cosmetic surgery is a practical way to boost self-esteem and happiness, asserts Michelle Copeland in the following viewpoint. While people are often accused of being vain, shallow, or even morally corrupt for wanting to have cosmetic surgery, an improved physical appearance is good for one's mental health and sense of well-being, contends Copeland. A youthful and healthy look also improves one's chances of being hired and of having a higher income, she points out. Copeland, a plastic surgeon, is author of Change Your Looks, Change Your Life.

As you read, consider the following questions:

1. According to a recent *People* magazine poll, what percentage of women were satisfied with their bodies?

2. What did the author's thirty-eight-year-old patient mean when she said, "Plastic surgery isn't just about beauty. It's about power"?

3. In Copeland's opinion, what are some of the legitimate body-image issues that should be addressed by plastic surgery?

Take a long, honest look in the mirror. You can do it for real (turn on that harsh overhead light and peel off some clothing), but my bet is you've done it often enough to know what it is about your body or face that you'd like to change.

What is it, for you? Maybe you've caught sight of that wattle that blurs your chin line (or, worse, that hangs over your crisp white collar) too many times. Maybe it's the crow's-feet that grab makeup and make a spray of fright lines at the corners of your eyes. Maybe it's your nose or earlobes, both of which sag as we age. Maybe it's your "Hi Janes" (the fleshy underside of the arm that continues to wiggle after you've stopped waving hello to your friend Jane); do they make you avoid wearing your favorite sleeveless blouse or halter top? Maybe it's your breasts—how far down has gravity pulled them? Maybe it's your stomach—are you willing to expose your midriff? (Perhaps you're currently carrying too much weight, once carried too much weight and your skin just hasn't got the message yet, or were never able to pull things up and together after your last pregnancy.) Maybe it's your hips: Is there no A-line skirt out there that can hide hips that bear witness to every Krispy Kreme [donut] you've wolfed down? Maybe it's those pesky spider veins, crisscrossing the backs of your legs like road maps of the East Coast. I could go on and on.

Perhaps you recognized yourself in one of these complaints, or more than one. If misery loves company, then at least you'll be happy to know that virtually everyone sees a problem or three when looking in the mirror.

That's the bad news. But we're positive thinkers here, and we're going to leave harsh reality behind. Instead, let's conjure that wonderful phrase again: "What if?"

Change Is Within Your Power

What if you could wave a wand and change *just one part* of your body—what would it be? (Forget whether it's practical, reasonable, or defensible, or whether anyone—including your own judgmental self—would "approve.") Now ask yourself something else: How many times in the last week have you thought about your nose, or crow's-feet, or wattle, or saddle-bags? How many times in the last day? How many times have you thought about that "flaw" in the last five years?

Now ask yourself how your life might have been different, in big ways or small, in the last five years if you hadn't been self-conscious about this part of yourself. How might your attitude about yourself have been different? How might this have had a ripple effect on the rest of your life?

The way we see ourselves and believe we're perceived by others is tied up with the way we look. Call it shallow, label it politically incorrect, swear that real beauty is on the inside . . . but, like it or not, looks matter. Beauty has always been a powerful stimulus and motivator: Throughout history, across all cultures, people have loaded themselves down with uncomfortable jewelry, submitted to body piercing and tattooing, worn outrageous wigs, and squeezed themselves into constricting corsets, clothes, and shoes, all in slavish pursuit of their culture's ideal of beauty. Today, in every area of our lives—at work, while socializing, in the public eye—attractive people consistently get more attention than their acne-scarred, overweight, receding-chinned counterparts. What's worse, our culture is obsessed with celebrity, and the mass media multiply and magnify examples of human "perfection" every day. In such an environment, how tough is it to "just be yourself" and like it? (In a recent *People* magazine poll, an anemic 10 percent of women said they were satisfied with their bodies.) Add to all this an aging population with expectations (realistic or not) of prolonged youth. It's a marvel that everyone but two or three well-adjusted supermodels isn't wracked by feelings of inadequacy and low self-esteem.

The pressure is often felt most intensely in the workplace. Studies show that traditionally good-looking people are perceived as smarter and friendlier than others; they make more money, and are *five times* more likely to be hired. But this isn't a recent phenomenon: Even the ancient Greek philosopher Aristotle once said that "Beauty is better than all letters of recommendation." With the continuing influx of women and corporate downsizing making work environments more competitive than ever, there's increased pressure to look polished—*and* youthful. One of my patients, a thirty-eight-year-old publishing executive on whom I performed a neck and forehead lift, describes the pressure this way:

> *In my profession I constantly interact with people, and I believe maintaining my looks gives me an edge. I'm not talking about being movie-star beautiful—who can be?—but I feel that appearing well put together, energetic, and youthful earns people's respect and attention, and ultimately gives me greater credibility. I am convinced looks make you money, so I think of surgery as an investment. Plastic surgery isn't just about beauty. It's about power.*

"Plastic surgery isn't just about beauty. It's about power." By allowing you to make subtle but important changes to your looks when and how *you* want, cosmetic surgery is a valuable, low-risk investment in your future health, happiness, and well-being.

One Woman Gets to "Yes"

Take Martha, for example. When the elegant sixty-three-year-old volunteer worker came in for an appointment, she told me she'd grown tired of striding confidently into a room, only to catch a glimpse of her reflection in a nearby mirror and feel that confidence disappear. "I just don't feel as tired and as old as I think I look," she said, despairingly.

I saw what Martha meant. While her voice projected energy and sharpness, she looked weary and her face was drawn. Yet she was reluctant to sign on for a cosmetic procedure, mostly for philosophical reasons. She felt that getting a face-lift was self-indulgent and a betrayal of her feminist beliefs. Her therapist, in fact, had counseled her *not* to seek a surgical remedy, urging her instead to deal with who she was and to accept her "limitations." Martha was too embarrassed even to discuss the issue with her grown children for fear that they would judge her harshly.

I pointed out to her that getting a face-lift, far from being a cop-out or an act of denial, can in fact be an effective, life-affirming way to embrace who you genuinely are. Although Martha's face did not reflect how she felt about herself, her negative feelings about how aging had diminished her spirit were absolutely valid. Should she have simply discounted her unhappiness? Of course not—and I think even her therapist would agree with that.

When Martha showed up two weeks later for a second consultation, she told me she'd come to see that wanting to look more attractive and vibrant was a worthy and respectable goal. "I'm confident in who I am, and my decision can't compromise that," she said. She had told her children about her plans, and was surprised at how supportive they were. Even I was astonished when she made the appointment for her surgery and asked for the works: forehead, eyes, neck, cheeks, lips! I won't say that Martha was anxiety-free: As the pre-surgery anesthesia was administered, she whispered to me, "I'm a liberal person by nature, but please be conservative!" Still, her feelings afterward spoke volumes: Martha was thrilled with the results, and she's confident she made the right move by taking control of her looks. And, happily, she's stopped avoiding mirrors. . . .

The Questions Every Patient Asks . . . and the Answers

Q: *"Am I just being vain?"*

A: Many people think that if you care about your appearance so much that you'd have plastic surgery done, then you're sinful or morally bankrupt. But why? Despite the increasing popularity of plastic surgery—according to the American Society for Aesthetic Plastic Surgery (ASAPS), 8.5 million cosmetic procedures were performed in the year 2001, an amazing 50 percent increase over the previous year, with baby boomers between thirty-five and fifty having the most work done—the skepticism and disapproval it can provoke still makes me marvel. This is especially so when so many of us, every single day, do all sorts of *other* things to make ourselves look better and feel younger. We diet. We color our hair. We whiten our teeth. We hire personal trainers. We spend billions yearly on over-the-counter skin-care products. We pop vitamins. We take hormone supplements. We get hair implants. We get facials. We take Viagra. Yet so many of us hesitate at the prospect of reaching these same goals with plastic surgery. Why?

Some believe it's "unnatural" to change one's body. Many feminists accuse women who opt for plastic surgery of caving in to male standards of beauty, or to the cult of youth. Other people argue that it's a hopeless gesture, external and superficial, that is only holding back the tides of the inevitable. But wanting to improve your appearance doesn't make you frivolous or superficial. In fact . . . there are manifestly *practical* reasons to maintain or improve your looks, from enhancing your earning power to staving off depression to actually improving the functioning of your body's largest organ—your skin. Is it vain to want to eliminate bags from under the eyes, especially when it can be done quickly, inexpensively, and with minimal recovery time? For men who've sported goatees since puberty, is it vain to want to fix that weak chin and stop hiding behind facial hair? For women embarrassed to wear fitted pants, is it vain to want to get rid of those saddlebags? For people chronically unhappy with their midsection, is it vain to want a waist that's more pleasing and youthful?

Perhaps. But if you're worried about being stigmatized, don't: In a recent study conducted by the American Association of Retired Persons (AARP), six of ten Americans over age fifty claim they'd have cosmetic surgery if they could, and more than three in four say they wouldn't be embarrassed if they had a procedure done and others found out about it.

Still, I understand how it's hard for many cosmetic surgery candidates to let go of the long-held belief that such a solution is narcissistic and undeserved. Sylvia, a fifty-year-old lawyer who comes to me regularly for microdermabrasion and light laser treatments, two skin-smoothing procedures, once confessed that she wanted to have her nose done. Yet the kind of person who gets a nose job could not possibly, in her view, be a modest, level-headed person who had achieved success through smarts, not looks—in other words, exactly the traits Sylvia saw in herself.

So what kicked her into gear? A colleague had recently confided in her that she'd had work done on her eyes and neck. The colleague looked terrific, and Sylvia couldn't believe the visible results, or the very idea of her having the procedure. "She's the last person on earth you would ever suspect would have something done!" Sylvia told me. "She's never fussed over her appearance, whether it's her clothes, hair, or makeup." Just seeing the results of a friend whom she respected, someone who was anything but a diva about her looks, gave Sylvia the courage to view things differently and schedule a nose job. Today Sylvia, the level-headed lawyer, has a smaller, less severe nose, and she says that the surgery has made a huge difference in how people look at her (literally!), as well as in how she sees herself.

Most patients who worry that they're being vain have legitimate body-image issues that they need to address. I hear the following all the time:

- "I feel as if my looks have aged, though I still feel young at heart."

- "I do anything to avoid revealing a physical flaw—like wearing baggy clothes or covering up a bathing suit, styling my hair a certain way, or refusing to wear open necks."

- "I've become increasingly self-conscious about my appearance."

- "I think my looks interfere with my being taken seriously at work, or may have held me back in my career."

- "At one time or another, someone—a spouse, friend, co-worker, even a stranger—has made negative comments about a physical flaw of mine, or referred to that feature in a way that undermined my confidence."

- "These days I flat-out refuse to undress in front of my partner or to make love with the lights on."

If even one of these statements sounds familiar, then toss out any notion that you're being frivolous. *When how you feel about your looks regularly affects your mood, confidence, relationships, or career, the problem is more than skin-deep. And if there's a solution that will help diminish or eliminate the problem, seeking that solution is hardly an act of vanity.* It's an act of practicality and common sense, and it's an important sign of your willingness to be pro-active about your own mental health and emotional well-being. In short, it's what you would do without hesitation about any other problem in your life.

Periodical Bibliography

The following articles have been selected to supplement the diverse views presented in this chapter.

Anna Arroba	"The Medicalization of Women's Bodies in the Era of Globalization," *Women's Health Journal*, January–March 2003.
Linda Bickerstaff	"Tattoos: Fad, Fashion, or Folly?" *Odyssey*, May 2005.
Rose Cooper	"Tattoo You?" April 12, 2006, www.online opinion.com.
Andy Crouch	"Wrinkles in Time: Botox Injections as a Spiritual Discipline," *Christianity Today*, August 2000.
Debra Darvick	"Service with a Smile," *Newsweek*, July 12, 2004.
GP	"The Price of Adornment," September 13, 2004.
Theresa E. Gunter and Betsy M. McDowall	"Body Piercing: Issues in Adolescent Health," *Journal for Specialists in Pediatric Nursing*, April–June 2004.
Bruce Jancin	"Body Modification: Personal Art or Cry for Help?" Family Practice News, August 15, 2005.
Jeremy Laurance	"Body Piercing Revival Is 'Rite of Passage' as well as Fashion," *The Independent*, March 8, 2003.
Polly Sparling	"Think Before You Ink," *Current Health 2: A Weekly Reader Publication*, October 2004.
Teen Vogue	"Hole Truth," April 2006.
Pippa Wysong	"Modified: Are Piercings and Tattoos Safe?" *Current Health 2: A Weekly Reader Publication*, March 2006.

OPPOSING
VIEWPOINTS®
SERIES

CHAPTER 3

What Triggers Self-Mutilation?

Chapter Preface

For two years, Adrian of Albuquerque, New Mexico, used razors, knives, and screwdrivers to make cuts on his legs and upper thighs. Many mornings he would wake up with his pajamas stuck to the clotted wounds. Then he'd pull off the clothing to let the blood flow again. "I can't get over how much I enjoyed it," he admitted in a 2006 *Albuquerque Tribune* article. "I loved waking up in the morning and seeing that I had done something to myself." But on July 6, 2005, Adrian cut himself so badly that he had to go to the hospital. He had to hold the deep horizontal leg wounds together with his hands as he limped to his parents' room to ask for help. "I cut myself so deep I required staples," he explained.

Adrian's cutting was a consequence of his depressive and anxiety disorders, which were diagnosed when he consulted a psychiatrist and a therapist. His self-injurious behavior was triggered by a need to "cut through" the numbness that often characterizes depression or borderline-personality disorder. With these kinds of emotional disturbances, people often cope by suppressing the inner turmoil and pain that they feel eventually shutting down their ability to feel anything. Self-injury provides a way to "kick-start" sensation when the numbness becomes too threatening. The physical pain becomes preferable to the feeling of emptiness and unreality.

Other self-injurers report the opposite: their emotional pain is in itself so overwhelming that they need some kind of a release valve to calm themselves down during a crisis. During a physical injury the brain releases endorphins, chemicals that relieve pain and that can even induce euphoria. Thus, self-injury can ironically become a way to soothe emotional pain and create a "high"—which makes it potentially addictive for repeat self-harmers.

Whether it is to feel less or to feel more, self-injury is a maladaptive coping strategy. As therapist Margaret Paul explains, "When a teen or young adult has not learned healthy ways of managing . . . intense feelings, they turn to physical pain as a way to blot out the emotional pain or gain a sense of control over the pain they feel. In a strange way, they are really not trying to hurt themselves—they are trying to protect themselves from something even more painful than the physical pain."

Unmanageable inner turmoil and mental illness are not the only triggers for self-injury. As the authors in the following chapter point out, social and cultural factors—such as images in the media, domestic violence, and cultural oppression—also play a role in this disturbing phenomenon. The common thread among all of these triggering factors, however, is the individual's inability to cope with overwhelming emotional distress in a healthy way.

> *"The constant barrage of pretty, perfect images on MTV [and] in fashion magazines are partly to blame for girls' uneasy relationships with their evolving bodies."*

Unrealistic Images in the Media Contribute to Self-Mutilation

Teen Vogue

In the following viewpoint the editors of Teen Vogue *maintain that self-mutilators are often perfectionists who demand a lot of themselves. In a world that places a high priority on appearance, young people, especially young women, may seek release from painful feelings of self-consciousness and self-hatred by injuring themselves. Some experts argue that the unrealistic images of beauty often seen in the media and fashion industry play a role in this self-harming behavior among women.* Teen Vogue *is a monthly fashion and entertainment magazine.*

As you read, consider the following questions:

1. How does clinical director Wendy Lader respond to the question of fake self-injury?

2. What is the relationship between self-injury and social anxiety, according to *Teen Vogue?*

3. What purposes do cutting and eating disorders serve, according to journalist Marilee Strong?

Her real name isn't Mandy Barquin, but that's what she calls herself on the Web site. It's a cyber bulletin board dedicated to a topic that, in the off-line world, gets lip service at best. "Cutting and depression, please help!" her post pleads. "I'm seventeen years old and my friend has recently taken up cutting."

Mandy's friend is a straight-A student. And so is Mandy. "I was number one in my class," she says. On paper, her life sounds, if not sitcom-perfect, at least above average. "We aren't bad off," she adds. "We don't have family problems. But last year, I was dating my ex-boyfriend and felt really stressed, and I was like, I don't know. I'd just gotten a job where I didn't like my boss I still don't like my boss," she giggles. "All the stress combined. I felt like a little ant. Like I was all alone." So she began cutting her legs. That's really obvious, especially in Florida, where you wear shorts. She had to come up with a litany of excuses for the etchings on her calves. "I said I got them in the bushes running after my little brother. Or that I fell on the picnic table at school."

Eventually, Mandy began slicing her arm, which, she points out, you can hide. When she got home from summer school, where she was taking extra credit classes, she would go into the bathroom and carve into herself with a pocketknife. The ritual calmed her, temporarily took her mind off her other problems. She didn't even mind the blood.

In her book *A Bright Red Scream* (Penguin), journalist Marilee Strong calls cutting the addiction of the nineties. But in 2004, the gory habit shows no sign of abating, especially among adolescent girls. And it isn't just pierced-and-tattooed goths or other self-identified outcasts who are employing

Unattainable Ideal?

Walk down the checkout aisle at the grocery store. Turn on the television for ten minutes. Flip through a fashion magazine, or look at the advertisements hanging in storefronts. It's pretty clear what a beautiful North American woman is supposed to look like. She's supposed to be tall and thin with perfect skin, voluptuous breasts, and long, flowing hair. But how many people do you know who actually look like this? The truth is that the female body you see on the front of that fashion magazine is an *unattainable* ideal.

It is a sad reality, but the look that so many women struggle so hard to obtain is unrealistic. All over North America, women and girls are starving themselves, exercising religiously, spending huge amounts of money, and hating their bodies for something that only exists in pictures.

Autumn Libal, Can I Change the Way I Look? *Broommall, PA: Mason Crest, 2005.*

shards of glass, penknives, scissors, anything sharp to turn their ulterior emotional pain into something undeniably physical. Cutters are often very sensitive, very creative, says Strong. They are often perfectionists, people who put high demands on themselves.

Of course, not everyone fits the profile. For some girls, cutting is a short-lived experiment. Like with drugs, some kids will try it to see what all the fuss is about, says Wendy Lader, clinical director of the S.A.F.E. Alternatives program near Chicago. Or, like Mandy (who stopped cutting when school started again), they hurt themselves temporarily to try to cope with a particularly stressful period in their life. Though cutters who run Web sites devoted to this form of self-injury often liken occasional cutting to amateur hour, Lader thinks it needs to be taken seriously. "People often ask me, Who are the real self-injurers and who are the fake ones?" she says. "I say I don't believe there is a fake self-injurer. If someone needs attention that badly, they have a problem. They don't feel like they're being seen or heard."

On the face of it, Jennifer,* a nineteen-year-old sophomore at a college in Westchester County, New York, has the opposite problem. She imagines that everyone is constantly checking her out. "Walking into a room where there's a lot of people, I get really nervous," she says. "I feel like time stops and everybody is looking at me, scrutinizing me." It's hard to blame her for feeling like Big Brother is watching. We live in a world where unflattering pictures secretly snapped by a phone cam can end up on the Web in minutes; where, thanks to reality TV, your next-door neighbor could end up on the cover of *Us Weekly*; or where a fight with your best friend could result in the revelation of your deepest, darkest secrets on her blog.

With so much pressure always to appear a certain way or else it's not surprising that Jennifer has, as she says, social anxiety issues. So you would think she'd blow off a Friday night party on campus to watch HBO in her dorm room. Or maybe she'd do the contrary: Become extra vigilant about her weight; dress up in all the right clothes; spend hours plucking and primping in front of the mirror.

Most unusually appearance-conscious people do one of two things: They hide from the glare of the spotlight or they accommodate it. But like Mandy, Jennifer took her discomfort in her skin literally, and so she did something else: She cut it.

"I couldn't handle emotions," she says. "And it was like a form of release. I didn't want to die. I just wanted release from the pain."

"My friends talk a lot about self-mutilation because of their anxiety. They feel self-conscious, like everyone is watching them," says Karen, who befriended Jennifer after noticing

* Name has been changed.

scars on her wrists that looked like Karen's own. But if girls feel like everyone is watching them, they don't sense that anyone is really seeing them, according to Lader. Cutters are trying to fill in the blanks and margins, to communicate more about themselves than they think blown-out blonde hair or a pair of Seven Jeans can. It's a way of attracting attention. "I think self-injurers believe they need to spice up the cover of the book so that someone might read it," says Lader, "even if that attention is ultimately negative."

And it may be easier than ever to cut yourself in this culture of casual cosmetic operations. The bloody slice-and-sews performed on TV shows like *I Want a Famous Face*, *Extreme Makeover*, and *Nip/Tuck* have turned plastic surgery into a spectator sport, numbing many of us to the sight of cutting into our own flesh. In her book *Female Perversions* (Jason Aronson Publishers), psychoanalyst Louise J. Kaplan posits that cutting is related to the painful, panic-ridden rituals women endure for the sake of beauty. Plucking, waxing, exfoliating: they're all attempts to make our bodies submit to ideas of what they should look like. But according to Kaplan, instead of ceding to a pair of tweezers or a grainy scrub in the hope that they'll help her appear pretty and feminine, a girl who cuts is doing just the opposite.

Strong thinks the constant barrage of pretty, perfect images on MTV in fashion magazines are partly to blame for girls' uneasy relationships with their evolving bodies. And the more girls disassociate from their physical selves, the more likely it is that they will find ways to physically hurt themselves. In fact, many girls who cut themselves are also anorexic or bulimic. Eating disorders and cutting serve similar purposes, says Strong, adding that many girls struggle with both. For people who experience self-hatred or alienation from their bodies, they are attempts to control the body, to punish the body. About 50 percent of cutters are victims of sexual abuse and may have never learned to accept their physicality. Puberty is a disturbing time, says Strong. Girls feel like the sexualization of their bodies increases their vulnerability to abuse. But with therapy, there is a way out. "Cutting is an attempt to communicate," says Lader. "The key is to try to put the emotions into words, not to distract yourself from them with pain."

"In a country where a female voice has
little importance, self-immolation is ...
a woman's way of shouting to the world
that her life is unbearable."

Cultural Oppression
Can Trigger Self-Mutilation

Kimberly Sevcik

*There has been an alarming increase in self-immolation among
women living in Afghanistan, reports Kimberly Sevcik in the following viewpoint. Some analysts attribute this increase to an influx of Western culture into a society that had recently been
ruled by a government that sanctioned oppression against
women. Afghan women still face subjugation, and their awareness of this oppression is heightened when they learn of the free-
doms and rights that Western women enjoy. In acts of desperation, some of these women set themselves on fire to protest against
the abuses they face at home and in their culture. Sevcik is a
freelance writer.*

As you read, consider the following questions:

1. According to the author, what led Shakila to set herself
   on fire?

2. How many self-inflicted burn victims were treated at Herat Public Hospital between November 2001 and February 2003, according to Dr. Abdul Azizi?

3. Why are some young Afghan burn victims afraid to admit that they self-immolated, according to Azizi?

On a stiflingly hot afternoon, 27-year-old Shakila Azizi is wheeled into the burn ward of Herat Public Hospital in western Afghanistan. As many as 20 women lie on the thin vinyl mattresses that line the ward, enveloped by metal cages covered with sheets. Nothing can touch these patients' raw, marbled skin: The risk of infection is too great.

Every bed is taken, so a nurse parks Shakila in the dimly lit corridor. Shakila's entire body is charred black, including some of her face. Emergency-room physicians estimate that she has burned 95 percent of her body—burns so deep that her purple veins stand out like highways on a road map. Only the soles of her feet are unscathed. "Allah, Al-lah," Shakila wails over and over. "Please, someone help me."

Her cries drift down the hall and into the crowded ward, where mothers, sisters, and husbands help the other patients sip juice through straws. Soon, the other patients' aunts and grandmothers cluster around Shakila, morbidly curious. "How is my skin?" Shakila asks anxiously. "What does it look like?" "It's fine," one woman assures her. The women exchange sidelong glances, clicking their tongues, shaking their heads.

Some of the patients in the burn ward are victims of accidental gas-stove explosions and fires ignited by toppled oil lamps. But in the past two years, there has been an epidemic of women who have deliberately set themselves on fire. In a country where a female voice has little importance, self-immolation is a desperate cry for attention, a woman's way of shouting to the world that her life is unbearable.

Shakila's Story

The morning had started like too many others for Shakila: Once again, her mother-in-law criticized her. The tea wasn't hot enough, the cup not clean enough. "Wash it again," her mother-in-law ordered, smacking the side of Shakila's head. Shakila returned with a clean cup, but her mother-in-law continued to berate her. "You're a lazy daughter-in-law," she taunted. "You're a bad wife."

The torment became too much for Shakila, who finally dared to yell back. She told her mother-in-law and sister-in-law how miserable she was in their household, how happy she and her husband, Noorullah, had been living alone in Iran the year before. As she spoke, Noorullah appeared. Mortified that his wife would show such disrespect to his mother, he removed his sandal and hit Shakila several times.

In tears by now, Shakila yelled that if the three of them didn't stop persecuting her, she would set herself on fire. She'd heard stories on the radio about women who'd self-immolated: women unhappily married to men 30 years their senior; women like her, living with extended families who treated them as servants.

"Go ahead," her sister-in-law challenged. Shakila vanished into the kitchen. Minutes later, she dashed through the house shrieking, her body engulfed in flames.

Later, at the hospital, Shakila tells the nurses that she hadn't really wanted to set herself on fire. "I was sure someone would stop me," she says. "But no one did."

An Epidemic of Self-Inflicted Burns

Although there are no exact numbers on how many women in Herat province have self-immolated, Dr. Abdul Aziz, an assistant doctor at the hospital, estimates between November 2001 and February 2003, the staff treated somewhere between 300 and 400 women with self-inflicted burns. "During the Taliban regime, there were almost no cases like this," he says. "Now, there are two or three burned women admitted each week."

Some medical workers attribute the increase, at least in part, to the sudden infiltration of Western culture. The young women setting themselves on fire grew up without knowing how much freedom women in other parts of the world enjoy. Now that every other house in Herat has a satellite dish (made of recycled soda cans), images of independent, carefree women enter their homes daily. Despite all the U.S. government's rhetoric about liberating Afghan women by deposing the Taliban, women are still subject to the same oppressive traditions that have plagued them for years. Some are mistreated when husbands take second wives, and although some women have returned to the workforce, the majority are still confined to their homes. When a woman marries, she generally moves into her husband's family's home. If the family is kind, she will be well cared for; if not, she is expected to swallow her despair. A woman who seeks outside counsel brings dishonor to her husband and family, in a culture where honor is everything.

"Women here have no social outlet, no place they can go to talk to other women [about] their problems," says Fatima Gailani, an Afghan women's rights advocate. "The frustration accumulates for months or years; they reach a hysterical moment, and they do the first thing that comes to mind—this thing they have all been hearing about. They burn themselves."

From the Trivial to the Tragic

The problem is so common that everyone seems to have a neighbor, a friend's daughter, a cousin, who has set herself on fire. Explanations range from the trivial to the tragic: One woman burned herself because her future mother-in-law pressured her to buy a wedding gown she didn't like; another, because her parents forbade her to leave the house alone.

What begins as a dramatic form of protest almost always results in death. "Women who douse themselves in kerosene generally burn more than 50 percent of their bodies," says Dr. Mohamed Humayoon Azizi, chief surgeon at the hospital's burn ward. "Our hospital doesn't have temperature-controlled rooms to stop the burns from deepening, and we don't have the capacity to do skin grafts, so it's difficult for us to save women with such severe burns."

The Aftermath

By her fourth day in the hospital, Shakila looks slightly better—the skin on her face has blistered and has begun to peel; at times, she can talk without moaning or writhing. But there are also moments when she feels like parts of her body have turned to stone. That's when she cries for her mother, who at that moment is driving the 20 hours from Iran to Herat.

Shakila's husband, Noorullah, keeps vigil at her bedside, adjusting her pillows, smoothing her hair. He feeds her bits of watermelon, which she struggles to keep down. When Dr. Azizi has to cut away the dead flesh on Shakila's calf to find a working vein for her IV, Noorullah hovers anxiously beside him. Beneath the surface of Shakila's skin, the tissue is white, as if her blood had just dried up and turned to dust.

Each night, once Shakila's painkillers have kicked in and she has drifted off to sleep, Noorullah prostrates himself on the sidewalk outside the hospital and prays. Usually, he sleeps on the linoleum floor just outside the women's ward, curled up beneath a sheet.

Back at Noorullah's parents' house, his and Shakila's two young sons, both under the age of 2, doze on the floor. When they wake, they cry for their mother, and nothing and no one can placate them.

Numbers Higher than Reported

While only three out of the 16 patients being treated in the burn ward have confessed to self-immolating, nurses and doctors speculate that the number is higher. For example, there is

Acts of Desperation

Ahmad Bassir is a Herat-based correspondent for Radio Free Afghanistan. He says women see no difference between their lives now and under the Taliban, and that desperation drives them to attempt suicide.

"They say we were hoping that after the fall of Taliban and after the transitional authority took power, the situation would improve for women, and there would be fewer restrictions. But we see that there have been no changes, and women are using this very violent act [of self-immolation] to show their protest. Most of these girls are literate, they are knowledgeable, and several of them are students," Bassir said.

Bassir adds that the despair is especially strong among women who once lived as refugees in neighboring Iran, where women enjoy far greater rights.

Golnaz Esfandiari,
"Self-Immolation of Women on the Rise in Western Provinces,"
March 1, 2004, www.rawa.org.

21-year-old Fauza, whose frantic relatives appeared at the hospital asking for "the woman who set herself on fire," and 17-year-old Suhaila, who burned 85 percent of her body—ostensibly in a gas-stove accident.

"Women who have burns all over their bodies are usually self-immolation cases," explains Dr. Azizi. "Victims of accidents tend to burn just one portion of the body." Dr. Azizi says that some girls are reluctant to admit that their burns are self-inflicted, partly out of shame and partly due to the mistaken fear that doctors will refuse to treat them: "In Islam, suicide is considered a sin."

Marzia's Plight

In one corner of the ward is a young girl of 14 or 15 years—she's not sure which—named Marzia. If it weren't for Marzia's sister-in-law, who is caring for her, the hospital might not know she had self-immolated. When the subject is raised, Marzia begins to whimper and talk about her pain.

Five weeks ago, Marzia plugged in the television that her husband had recently brought home, and it short-circuited. Because it was the first television she had ever owned, Marzia believed that it was beyond repair. "My husband had worked for months to buy that TV, and I felt awful," she says. Terrified at the prospect of her husband's wrath, she set herself on fire.

Marzia's face is still beautiful, her skin smooth and tawny to the base of her chin. From her neck to her pelvis, however, the skin is a furious red, rough with scabs. Dr. Azizi says that Marzia has burned only 45 percent of her body, making her one of the more fortunate patients.

Though Marzia will survive, Dr. Azizi says she will have limited use of her arms and torso, and her head will be frozen in a downward-gazing position. Every morning, Marzia walks up and down the hospital corridor to keep her joints flexible. Wrapped in a stained sheet, her shoulders hunched, her face hidden, her gait staccato, Marzia could easily be mistaken for a woman five times her age.

A Response to Abuse

Shakila is just beginning to laugh again, she is just feeling the stirrings of an appetite, when another patient is whisked into the burn ward. She is in even worse shape than Shakila, the doctors whisper. Fatonah Khairkhowa's body is 100-percent burned.

Fatonah is an elementary-school teacher at one of Herat's freshly minted girls' schools, and a graduate student at Herat University. But her education has not protected her from domestic violence. "For 13 years, Fatonah's husband beat her,"

her sister, Hatifah Khairkhowa, says. "Every time I saw her, she had a new bruise or cut." Fatonah confided in her colleagues about her husband's abuse, but they felt powerless. "We knew that if she sought outside help, the abuse would intensify," says a fellow teacher, Seema Gurzwani. Although domestic abuse is illegal in Afghanistan, says Seema, it is rare for men to be jailed for beating their wives.

For years, Fatonah debated whether to leave her husband. But under Islamic law, in cases of divorce, fathers get custody of children over the age of 7, which meant Fatonah would lose two of their children: a 9-year-old daughter and a 12-year-old son. "I chose my children's lives over mine," she says.

The day that Fatonah burned herself, she'd gone to the bazaar in the morning; at lunchtime, when she returned, her husband castigated her for dallying, and they argued. He told her he would deal with her later. That night, he pressed his knee into her stomach and wrapped his hands around her neck until she gasped for air. Fatonah flailed, hit him in the face, and crawled away. First, she tried electrocuting herself; then, she poured kerosene over her body and lit a match.

On her first day in the hospital, Fatonah is flooded with visits from colleagues and relatives: majestic, articulate women who peel back their burkas to look into the doctors' eyes as they bombard them with questions: "What percentage of her body is burned?" "What are her chances of survival?"

Family Anguish

Because of Fatonah's high standing in the community, the incident alarms city officials. An investigator from the Human Rights Commission shows up at the hospital. The police arrest Fatonah's husband. The public television station airs a half-hour show about her case and the self-immolation issue in general, in which the province's governor, Ismail Khan, expresses his concern. "We can no longer think of [self-immolation] as a problem of illiteracy and ignorance," he says.

Fatonah's family considers taking her to Pakistan or Iran for better treatment. But Dr. Azizi advises against it: Her body is exceedingly vulnerable to infection. "As soon as she can walk, it will be fine for you to take her," Dr. Azizi says. Then he takes her brother-in-law aside and tells him the truth: "I am sorry," he says, "but Fatonah will not reach that point. She is dying."

The next day, Fatonah's children come to see her. Her 3-year-old immediately begins to sob and is carried off by an aunt. Her older son and daughter crouch by the bed. They peer into their mother's face, covered with antibiotic cream, and ask how she's feeling. "Fine," she lies. They ask when she will come home. "Soon, my dear ones," she lies again. "When I am better, we will go to live with your auntie in the United States."

The children nod solemnly, then retreat into the hallway, swiping at their tears.

It's been six days since Shakila entered the burn ward. Her mother, Nooria, has finally arrived from Iran, and she kneels by her daughter's bed, trying to make her smile. Only when Shakila is out of earshot does Nooria's grief emerge. "What has happened to my beautiful daughter?" she says, struggling to stifle her sobs. Then grief shifts into anger. "Shakila's in-laws drove her to do this," she shouts. The visitors in the ward turn to stare. "If they were here, I would set them all on fire!"

By the next evening, Shakila is gasping for air. It's not un-expected, given the severity of her burns. Her blood flow has slowed and oxygen can't reach her lungs, and her torso and hands are immobile. Noorullah paces the corridor, his hand on his heart; then he settles in a chair beside her and speaks to her in whispers, his face inches from hers. "Maybe this is our fate," he says. "Maybe this is what God wanted." Hours slip by. The late-afternoon sun fills the room, then disappears. The sound of an imam calling worshippers to evening prayer drifts through the burn ward.

Noorullah sits at Shakila's bedside with his face pressed into his palm. Slowly, she shifts her eyes toward him. She opens her mouth to talk, but no words escape. She raises her arm from the mattress and moves it half an inch in his direction. Another half an inch. Another. It hovers in the air for a minute, quivering, then drops to the mattress.

The next day, her bed is empty.

| "Self-harm [is] rooted in child and adult experiences of violence and abuse."

Domestic Abuse Can Trigger Self-Mutilation

Cathy Fillmore, Colleen Anne Dell, and Elizabeth Fry

Cathy Fillmore, Colleen Anne Dell, and Elizabeth Fry have conducted research on the connections between female self-harm, domestic abuse, and social position. In the following viewpoint, these authors discuss the results of one such study on Canadian women who had also been in conflict with the law. They conclude that the potential for self-injury is strongest among women who grew up in unstable families and who have been subjected to child abuse and domestic violence.

As you read, consider the following questions:

1. According to a 1995 study cited by the authors, what percentage of federally sentenced Canadian women have commited self-injury?

2. What did the women who participated in the authors' study claim to be the strongest risk factors for self-harm?

3. What are the most effective responses to the problem of self-injury, according to the authors?

The study on which this article is based, "Prairie Women, Violence and Self-Harm," examined the connection between the critical events in childhood and adult life of women who inflict harm on themselves (self-harm) and their social position.

The increase in the number of women in conflict with the law who harm themselves is alarming. A 1995 study found that 59 percent of women in Canada sentenced for federal offences have committed self-injury. Although the link between childhood experience of abuse and violence and self-harm is widely acknowledged, the intersection of self-harm with adult experiences of violence and abuse, and one's social position is frequently overlooked.

A Study on Abuse and Self-Harm

For the study, 44 women with a history of being in conflict with the law were interviewed. Some of them live in the community, others, in correctional institutions. Aboriginal women comprised 64 percent of the sample, Caucasians, 32 percent, and others, 3 percent. Nine staff members in the community and correctional agencies were also interviewed. A focus group discussion was also held with six incarcerated women. In addition to a survey of correctional staff, several community service and correctional institution policies and practices on self-harm were reviewed.

The study found that adult experiences of violence and abuse—particularly partner abuse—were common among the women. An important finding is that some women linked abuse by their partners to self-harming behaviours and identified this abuse as a risk factor. Most of the women have a common experience of poverty—both material and social, and growing up in highly unstable and unsupportive families.

Self-Inflicted Violence as a Tool

Everyone assumes they know what SIV [self-inflicted violence] is about, although their theories are often wildly divergent and self-contradictory. We're doing it, we are told, for attention, or because we're addicted to pain, or because we are manipulative, or because we want to hurt our therapists, or because we're incorrigibly bad children, or because we are Borderline.... A few, a very few, have actually talked to women living with SIV, and have listened to what we say about our own lives, and know that the SIV has nothing to do with our therapists or labels and everything to do with being survivors of trauma, and of trying to survive the world-rocking aftershocks of rapes and battering and torture.... Seen as a coping tool for abuse survivors, SIV begins to make perfect sense.

Farar Elliott, Off Our Backs,
May 2001.

Another important finding is that both Aboriginal and non-Aboriginal women said they benefited from, and highly value, traditions from Aboriginal culture, and believe these traditions should be incorporated into programmes designed to address self-harm.

The Instability Factor

The women mirror the profile of a woman in conflict with the law in the Prairie region of Canada. The average age is 31 years, with grade 10 being the common educational level reached. Many of the women had been placed in various group and foster homes as youths. The majority revealed highly unstable and transient relationship patterns. The women had an average of two children, with most of the children living in foster care, group homes, or adopted out.

The likelihood of self-harm was strongest when the women were in highly unstable and unsupportive families and adult partnerships. Such families were characterised by: frequent moving and intermittent or permanent placements in foster and group homes; absent, weak, or traumatic bonds with primary caregivers (especially the mother); unmet emotional and social needs; and childhood abuse and violence (sexual, emotional, physical, and neglect). In the women's adult relationships, abuse and violence, primarily by a partner, were common.

Functions of Self-Harm

Both the women integrated into the community and those in detention identified partner abuse, loss of and separation from their children, isolation and loneliness as the leading risk factors for self-harm. However, for the women in detention, traumatic recollections of past child abuse were the critical risk factor that precipitated their conflict with the law.

Except for one, the women had experienced violence and abuse as an adult, primarily by a partner. "With your spouse, you're too scared [to fight back] sometimes," one woman said. "You've been hurt so many times, why not hurt yourself? 'There, I did it, you happy?'" The relationship between women's self-harm and partner violence is an important area obviously requiring further investigation.

The women mentioned several functions of self-harm that enabled them to survive and cope with the unbearable emotional pain and distress:

- To cope with an abusive partner
- To fill the need for attention and nurturing
- Self-punishment and self-blame
- To deal with isolation and loneliness
- To distract and deflect pain

- To release and cleanse oneself of pain

- To feel or bring oneself back to reality

- To express painful life experiences

- To control oneself

Although most of the functions of self-harm identified by the service providers corresponded to those identified by the women themselves, the former minimised the importance of some of the functions identified by the women, such as to meet the need for attention and nurturing and as a response to isolation and loneliness. From the service provider's perspective, moreover, the women's self-harm was a form of manipulation and a way to make the staff take control over them.

Effective Response

The women expressed a need for more opportunities to express and discuss their emotional pain and distress. In particular, they wanted recognition of their experience of abuse and violence, both in staff interaction and in the form of specific programmes. The women also cited a need for a deeper understanding and insight into their self-harming behaviours and to learn healthier, empowering coping mechanisms.

Both the women and the staff found Aboriginal approaches to healing helpful, and believed these would be an effective component of any programme to address self-harm. These traditional Aboriginal teachings, they said, offer a balanced and meaningful approach to self-recovery.

A common perception was that many of the current practices to prevent self-harm are inappropriate. Indeed, previous research indicates that the tendency toward self-harm increases with segregation and similar "punitive" measures, such as restraints, could re-traumatise women who have experienced childhood or adult violence.

The women interviewed also demonstrated personal agency and a creative capacity for identifying alternatives to self-harming behaviour. The women wrote in journals and engaged in vigorous physical activity. Daily smudging (burning sage as a cleansing ritual) was used to attend to spiritual needs. The women also turned to friends and partners, and sought individual counseling, peer support programming, group therapy and community agency support. Volunteer work, babysitting and other activities that allowed the women to feel they were making a contribution were also identified as helpful responses.

Clearly, a holistic, woman-centred approach to eliminate self-harm is necessary. This requires, however, not only the recognition of women's unique personal histories and biographies, but also an understanding of the social antecedents of self-harm that are rooted in child and adult experiences of violence and abuse. Women's self-harm cannot be separated from their social contexts and structures.

| "When someone engages in self-harm, they may have a variety of intentions."

A Variety of Factors Can Trigger Self-Mutilation

Laura E. Gibson

A number of factors may influence an individual's self-harming behavior, explains Laura E. Gibson in the following viewpoint. Self-injurers often report having histories of childhood abuse or neglect; they also tend to have higher rates of certain other kinds of psychological problems, such as substance abuse or eating disorders. The author contends that the reasons people engage in self-harm include, among other things, a need to relieve emotional tension, a way to communicate pain, and a desire to punish themselves. Gibson is an assistant professor of psychology at the University of Vermont.

As you read, consider the following questions:

1. What are the most commonly reported self-harming behaviors, according to Gibson?
2. According to the author, self-harmers have higher rates of which psychological problems?
3. How does Gibson define Dialectical Behavior Therapy?

Laura E. Gibson, "Self-Harm Fact Sheet," *SIARI, www.siari.co.uk*, April 3, 2004. Reproduced by permission.

"Self-harm" refers to the deliberate, direct destruction of body tissue that results in tissue damage. When someone engages in self-harm, they may have a variety of intentions; these are discussed below. However, the person's intention is NOT to kill themselves. You may have heard self-harm referred to as "parasuicide," "self-mutilation," "self-injury," "self-abuse," "cutting," "self-inflicted violence," and so on.

How Common Is Self-Harm?

Self-harm is not well-understood and has not yet been extensively studied. The rates of self-harm revealed through research vary tremendously depending on how researchers pose their questions about this behavior. One widely cited estimate of the incidence of impulsive self-injury is that it occurs in at least 1 person per 1,000 annually. A recent [2004] study of psychiatric outpatients found that 33% reported engaging in self-harm in the previous 3 months. A recent study of college undergraduates asked study participants about specific self-harm behaviors and found alarmingly high rates. Although the high rates may have been due in part to the broad spectrum of self-harm behaviors that were assessed (e.g., severe scratching and interfering with the healing of wounds were included), the numbers are certainly cause for concern:

- 18% reported having harmed themselves more than 10 times in the past,

- 10% reported having harmed themselves more than 100 times in the past, and

- 38% endorsed a history of deliberate self-harm.

- The most frequently reported self-harm behaviors were needle sticking, skin cutting, and scratching, endorsed by 16%, 15%, and 14% of the participants, respectively.

It is important to note that research on self-harm is still in the early stages, and these rates may change as researchers begin to utilize more consistent definitions of self-harm and more studies are completed.

Who Engages in Self-Harm?

Only a handful of empirical studies have examined self-harm in a systematic, sound manner. Self-harm appears to be more common in females than in males, and it tends to begin in adolescence or early adulthood. While some people may engage in self-harm a few times and then stop, others engage in it frequently and have great difficulty stopping the behavior. Several studies have found that individuals who engage in self-harm report unusually high rates of histories of:

- Childhood sexual abuse

- Childhood physical abuse

- Emotional neglect

- Insecure attachment

- Prolonged separation from caregivers

At least two studies have attempted to determine whether particular characteristics of childhood sexual abuse place individuals at greater risk for engaging in self-harm as adults. Both studies reported that more severe, more frequent, or a longer duration of sexual abuse was associated with an increased risk of engaging in self-harm in one's adult years.

Also, individuals who self-harm appear to have higher rates of the following psychological problems:

- High levels of dissociation

- Borderline personality disorder

- Substance abuse disorders

- Posttraumatic stress disorder

- Intermittent explosive disorder

- Antisocial personality

- Eating disorders

While there are many theories about why individuals harm themselves, the answer to this question varies from individual to individual.

Some reasons why people engage in self-harm:

- To distract themselves from emotional pain by causing physical pain

- To punish themselves

- To relieve tension

- To feel real by feeling pain or seeing evidence of injury

- To feel numb, zoned out, calm, or at peace

- To experience euphoric feelings (associated with release of endorphins)

- To communicate their pain, anger, or other emotions to others

- To nurture themselves (through the process of healing the wounds)

How Is Self-Harm Treated?

Self-harm is a problem that many people are embarrassed or ashamed to discuss. Often, individuals try to hide their self-harm behaviors and are very reluctant to seek needed psychological or even medical treatment.

Because self-harm is often associated with other psychological problems, it tends to be treated under the umbrella of a co-occurring disorder like a substance abuse problem or an eating disorder. Sometimes the underlying feelings that cause the self-harm are the same as those that cause the co-occurring disorder. For example, a person's underlying feelings of shame may cause them to abuse drugs *and* cut themselves. Often, the self-harm can be addressed in the context of therapy for an associated problem. For example, if people can learn healthy coping skills to help them deal with their urges to abuse substances, they may be able to apply these same skills to their urges to harm themselves.

There are also some treatments that specifically focus on stopping the self-harm. A good example of this is Dialectical Behavior Therapy, a treatment that involves individual therapy and group skills training. DBT is a therapy approach that was originally developed for individuals with borderline personality disorder who engage in self-harm or "parasuicidal behaviors." Now the treatment is also being used for self-harming individuals with a wide variety of other psychological problems, including eating disorders and substance dependence. The theory behind DBT is that individuals tend to engage in self-harm in an attempt to regulate or control their strong emotions. DBT teaches clients alternative ways of managing their emotions and tolerating distress. Research has shown that DBT is helpful in reducing self-harm.

Pharmacological Treatments

It is possible that psychopharmacological treatments would be helpful in reducing self-harm behaviors, but this has not yet been rigorously studied. As yet, there is no consensus regarding whether or not psychiatric medications should be used in relation to self-harm behaviors. This is a complicated issue to study because self-harm can occur in many different populations and co-occur with many different kinds of psychological problems. If you are wondering about the use of medications for the emotions related to your self-harm behaviors, we recommend that you discuss this with your doctor or psychiatrist.

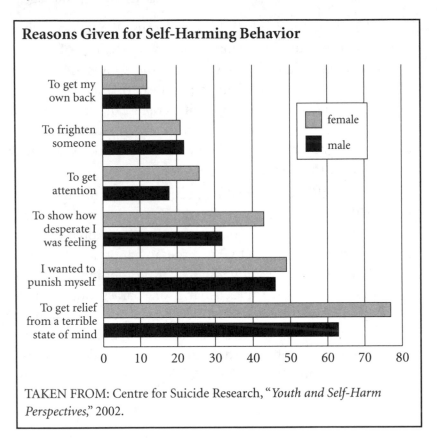

Reasons Given for Self-Harming Behavior

TAKEN FROM: Centre for Suicide Research, "*Youth and Self-Harm Perspectives,*" 2002.

If you are trying to find a psychologist or psychiatrist, we advise you to ask them whether they are familiar with self-harm. Consider which issues are important to you and make sure you can talk to the potential therapist about them. Remember that you are the consumer—you have the right to interview therapists until you find someone with whom you feel comfortable. You may want to ask trusted friends or medical professionals for referrals to psychologists or psychiatrists. Consider asking your potential provider questions, such as:

- How do you treat self-harm?

- What do you think causes self-harm?

- Do you have experience in treating self-harm?

For tips on communicating with medical providers in a medical context (including communicating with professionals in an emergency room), go to http://www.palace.net/~llama/psych/injury.html, click the icon on the left side of the screen that reads "first aid," and then click the icon "what to expect in the emergency room." For more ideas on finding a therapist who is familiar with the treatment of self-harm, go to http://www.palace.net/~llama/psych/injury.html and then click on "offline resources" on the left side of the screen. . . .

Support for Self Harmers

If you have a friend or relative who engages in self-harm, it can be very distressing and confusing for you. You may feel guilty, angry, scared, powerless, or any number of things. . . . Some general guidelines are:

- Take the self-harm seriously by expressing concern and encouraging the individual to seek professional help.

- Don't get into a power struggle with the individual—ultimately they need to make the choice to stop the behavior. You cannot force them to stop.

- Don't blame yourself. The individual who is self-harming initiated this behavior and needs to take responsibility for stopping it.

- If the individual who is self-harming is a child or adolescent, make sure the parent or a trusted adult has been informed and is seeking professional help for them.

- If the individual who is engaging in self-harm does not want professional help because he or she doesn't think the behavior is a problem, inform them that a professional is the best person to make this determination. Suggest that a professional is a neutral third party who will not be emotionally invested in the situation and so will be able to make the soundest recommendations.

"In many cases, borderline and factitious patients externalize their psychic
struggles by producing scars or other
tangible evidence of their internal conflict."

People Who Are Faking Illness
May Engage in Self-Mutilation

Marc D. Feldman

*In the following viewpoint, Marc D. Feldman discusses one little-
known cause of self-mutilation: factitious disorder, the term used
to describe a syndrome in which people create self-induced illnesses, often in order to assume status as a patient. Some people
with factitious disorder injure themselves to express deep internal
conflict or because they believe that suffering is beneficial. Others
may harm themselves to gain a feeling of control over abusers, or
to escape abuse. Yet another theory is that factitious patients
gain sympathy and self-esteem from having unusual illnesses
and injuries. Feldman, a physician, is the author of* Playing
Sick? Untangling the Web of Munchausen Syndrome, Munchausen by Proxy, Malingering, and Factitious Disorder.

As you read, consider the following questions:

1. What is the difference between the self-harm of people with borderline personality disorder and that of people with factitious disorder, according to Feldman?

2. What example does the author use to explain how factitious patients may injure themselves to escape abusive situations?

3. What is the self-enhancement hypothesis on factitious disorder, according to Feldman?

Doctors are trained to follow specific paths toward diagnosis and to scrutinize small pieces of information in reaching conclusions. But when dealing with factitious disorder, medical professionals must look at these patients in the broadest terms. They must overlook nothing, no matter how farfetched it may seem, that might contribute to answering the questions: "Who would do something like this, and why?"

Uncovering the Motivations

While borderline personality disorder is characterized by self-mutilation which the patient acknowledges, factitious behavior involves concealing the volition underpinning the self-abuse. Both can occur at the same time, or alternate in ways we can rarely predict. . . . The endurance of pain—often extreme in quality—is common to both borderline personality disorder and factitious disorder. Paradoxically, many patients with borderline personality and/or factitious disorder regard self-inflicted pain as positive, particularly pain that results from having misled physicians to perform complex surgical operations. The distorted thought processes of these patients are evident even in the way they speak about pain. One woman, after injecting herself with bacteria, created a horrendously painful bacterial infection in her spine. When recounting the ordeal which nearly claimed her life, she referred to her pain as *delicious*.

Since borderline and factitious disorder patients find that pain reminds them that they are real, pain has the effect of organizing them. They immediately become patients and there is no more ambiguity about the role they are to fulfill and who they are. It helps them define the boundaries of where they end and the world begins.

In many cases, borderline and factitious patients externalize their psychic struggles by producing scars or other tangible evidence of their internal conflict. This dynamic explains the horrifying and ultimately unnecessary disfigurement factitious patients are willing to undergo. Wendy Scott's arms, legs, and abdomen were grossly deformed by scarring so severe that experienced surgeons found themselves dumbfounded and appalled. Interestingly, in enduring pain some patients feel a primitive honor that is reminiscent of some tribal cultures. Many cultures admire and celebrate individuals who demonstrate stoicism while bearing great pain. In some tribal societies, rites of passage are based on endurance of extreme pain and even scarification (the creation of permanent scars that can cover the individual virtually from head to toe). Modern societies have their own version of delivering this message. Consider the recruiting commercials for the military that depict the pain-contorted faces of new recruits as eliminating weakness.

Spiritual Redemption

Those who continually feel bad about themselves, as borderline and factitious disorder patients generally do, believe not only that they deserve punishment but seek it with the avidity of the ancient ascetics (who carried pebbles in their shoes) and self-flagellants (who flogged themselves in service to God). . . . This recognition means that some people continue to believe that pain has spiritually redeeming qualities. Doctors are missing this moral component in some cases because, though we try not to, we always approach patients with preconceptions, one of which is that people would never want to be in pain.

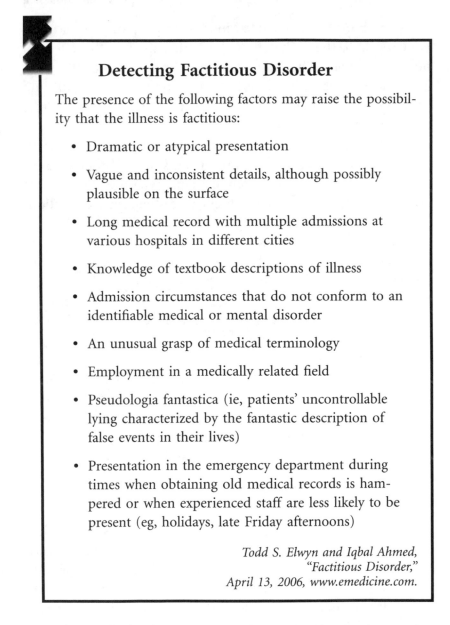

Detecting Factitious Disorder

The presence of the following factors may raise the possibility that the illness is factitious:

- Dramatic or atypical presentation

- Vague and inconsistent details, although possibly plausible on the surface

- Long medical record with multiple admissions at various hospitals in different cities

- Knowledge of textbook descriptions of illness

- Admission circumstances that do not conform to an identifiable medical or mental disorder

- An unusual grasp of medical terminology

- Employment in a medically related field

- Pseudologia fantastica (ie, patients' uncontrollable lying characterized by the fantastic description of false events in their lives)

- Presentation in the emergency department during times when obtaining old medical records is hampered or when experienced staff are less likely to be present (eg, holidays, late Friday afternoons)

Todd S. Elwyn and Iqbal Ahmed,
"Factitious Disorder,"
April 13, 2006, www.emedicine.com.

I am reminded of a woman who plunged a knife into her chest, barely missing her heart. She claimed to be a member of a religious group which didn't believe in any demarcation between life and death, so she couldn't understand why the doctors were anxious about her well-being and why we were talking about protracted hospitalization for psychiatric care. She really believed that her action was insignificant, and yet we were dismayed as a group of professionals. Even if patients earnestly say things like, "suffering is good for the soul," most doctors would dismiss that explanation instantly. Yet piety for tolerating pain may be an unconscious factor in some cases of factitious disorder. People do things all the time for reasons of which they are not aware, and their actions may be highly influenced by spiritual beliefs, even unconventional and subconscious ones.

Given sufficient time with a factitious disorder patient, which is rare because these patients typically flee, doctors may be able to pinpoint individual motivation, even if a person is unaware of the forces driving his or her false illness for instance, protective environments, such as hospitals, are hard to give up if a person is not used to feeling safe in life.

Abuse and Control

Some disease portrayals are fraught with elements of sadomasochism. In a sadomasochistic relationship, the abused person identifies with the abuser and the relationship becomes symbiotic. In kidnapping and prisoners-of-war cases there can also be an identification that occurs between captive and captor called the Stockholm syndrome. In 1974, four Swedes held in a bank vault for six days during a robbery became attached to their captors. According to psychologists, the abused bond to their abusers as a means to endure violence and fear. Similarly, adults with factitious disorder may identify with their childhood abusers and perpetuate through self-induced illness the physical abuse that they experienced as children. They may accept the idea that abuse is a normal part of living.

For patients who have suffered childhood abuse, control is a huge issue. They were not strong or powerful enough as children to control what was happening to them. As adults, they have unresolved rage that displays itself in highly controlling behaviors. For example, they may engineer for doctors to contribute to their abuse through unnecessary tests and surgeries. Even though it harms them, the patient may feel in control through this behavior. In childhood there was nothing this person could do about the physical punishment; now the patient can intensify or curtail it at whim.

Sexual abuse also provides a foundation for self-inflicted physical disorders. Much more research is needed in this area, but consider the case of a young girl who stuck her eyes with pins to escape continual rape by her father. Once she was seriously wounded, she was extricated from her painful environment. That was obviously an extraordinarily desperate way of ending the abuse.

Sometimes feigned illnesses have symbolic aspects that also suggest a background of sexual violation. Munchausen by proxy, for example, has some sexual overtones since instrumentation being applied to the body in some ways is a sexual act. And tampering with and handling another person's genitals, urine, and feces, and injecting substances into the body, all have sexual connotations.

Theories on Factitious Disorder

The kinds of *psychodynamic or psychoanalytic* hypotheses illustrated above are extremely useful in many cases and have a rich history. For those reasons, I have given them a lot of attention. However, they necessarily involve some conjecture about an individual's unconscious drives and are therefore difficult to prove.

In contrast, *behavioral* theories focus on observable responses rather than impute actions to unconscious impulses, conflicts, and defense mechanisms. Behaviorists often focus on the fact that many patients with factitious disorder have experienced a critical illness as children or had a relative who was seriously ill. These children may find it rewarding to experience or witness the sympathy, attention, encouragement, and affection that is accorded occupants of the "sick role." They may also be gratified that illness permits an avoidance of responsibilities and duties. Behavioral approaches conclude that this past social learning and reinforcement can influence children as they grow up and are expressed through illness deception. Behavioral perspectives contribute to our understanding of factitious illness behavior, but do not explain why most children with such backgrounds do not become high utilizers of health care.

Faulty cognitive processing is another theory. In this view, the patient perceives bodily sensations abnormally, misinterpreting normal physiological functions as alarming or dangerous. By frequently visiting physicians and undergoing physical examinations and procedures, the patient is reassured, albeit temporarily, that no health problems exist. A serious problem with the cognitive processing model is that it assumes that factitious disorder is ultimately guided by the patient's authentic worry about his or her health. In reality, disease forgers deliberately feign or produce signs and symptoms; they do not simply misperceive or misinterpret them.

A *biological/organic view* suggests that *abnormal brain anatomy and/or function* is at the root of some cases. This neuropsychiatric approach to feigned or induced illness is in its infancy, and testing is constrained by the shortage of research funds. In addition, there are ethical reasons not to subject patients to batteries of brain and other tests when continual testing is one of the problems that treatment seeks to overcome. There have been no genetic studies of medical deception. Brain imaging, specialized psychological testing, and brain-wave studies of these patients have been small in scale, and abnormalities observed in a minority of the patients are nonspecific—that is, these same findings appear in a wide range of conditions that have nothing to do with disease simulation or induction.

Social psychologist James C. Hamilton has advanced the so-called *self-enhancement hypothesis*. He and his colleagues have shown in several experiments that, curiously, some individuals made to believe that they have an unusual, if rather inconsequential, medical anomaly experience increased self-esteem as a result. They feel special and can even covet the prospect of being evaluated and treated by high-status physicians—people whom they might not otherwise meet. The creation of research settings in which to study subjects' thoughts and feelings represents an extraordinary advance in the field and holds great promise.

Periodical Bibliography

The following articles have been selected to supplement the diverse views presented in this chapter.

Matthew Akid — "Beneath the Scars," *Nursing Times*, July 16, 2002.

Economist — "Silent Scourge: Self Harming," October 28, 2006.

Farar Elliott — "'Self-Inflicted' Violence," *Off Our Backs*, May 2001.

Liza Finlay — "Aching for Affection," *Chatelaine*, October 2000.

Nicci Gerrard — "Why Are So Many Teenage Girls Cutting Themselves?" *The Observer*, May 19, 2002.

Liana Heitin — "'I Can't Stop Pulling Out My Hair!'" *Marie Claire*, May 2004.

Rebecca Jenkins — "Goth Culture Clue to Increased Self-Harm Risk," *Australian Doctor*, April 28, 2006.

Diana Keough — "Dark Salvation," *Plain Dealer*, January 9, 2005.

Jeffrey Kluger — "The Cruelest Cut: Often It's the One Teens Inflict on Themselves," *Time*, May 16, 2005.

John Monaghan — "Cather Hardwicke's *Thirteen* Captures Rebellious Kids' Lives," *Detroit Free Press*, August 29, 2003.

Christine Roberts — "'I Couldn't Stop Hurting Myself,'" *Good Housekeeping*, Septermber 1999.

Sue Vorenbeerg — "An Ugly Slice of Life," *Albuquerque Tribune*, February 6, 2006.

Jonathan E. Yoder — "'I Cut Myself, Doctor—But It Doesn't Look Quite Right," *Medical Economics*, May 8, 2000.

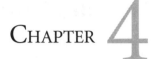

CHAPTER 4

What Should Be Done to Reduce Self-Injurious Behavior?

Chapter Preface

People generally engage in self-harming behavior as a way to cope with confusing and overwhelming emotions, and the thought of seeking help for their problem can become yet another emotional quandary. Young self-injurers especially worry about what others would think if their behavior were discovered. They either fear that they will not be understood or taken seriously—or that their problem will be perceived as so disturbing that they will be labeled as mentally ill or dangerous to others. As mental health expert Celia Richardson points out in a survey on self-harm,

> Many young people said they did not have anyone they felt they could talk to . . . They certainly didn't know how to contact support services. Some were worried that if they were open about their self-harm, this could affect their choices for the future: they were worried they wouldn't be able to work in professions such as teaching, nursing, or childcare because of perceptions that people who self-harm are dangerous and should not be allowed to work with children.

Analysts have learned that some of these fears have a basis in fact. People who go to emergency rooms because of a self-inflicted wound all too often receive unsympathetic treatment—and even punitive actions from nurses and other medical personnel. For example, self-harmers are sometimes scolded for being attention seekers or nuisances, and medical personnel may refuse to give them anesthesia while stitching their wounds. In addition, they might find themselves dismissed as time wasters and less deserving of care than other injured people. Researchers D. Jeffrey and A. Warm report that certain myths about intentional self-harm are not uncommon among emergency room personnel, including the notion that self-harmers are attention seekers who do not really want to be cured of their problem.

These attitudes among emergency personnel are, of course, counterproductive because they make it even less likely that self-injurers will seek out medical attention for their wounds or therapeutic assistance for their emotional problems. It also makes it more likely that self-injurers will continue their behavior in secret. Thus, one significant step toward reducing self-harming behavior, many experts argue, is to educate healthcare workers on the facts about self-harm in order to dispel prejudices and to encourage more compassionate, empathetic treatment of self-injurers who seek their assistance.

In the following chapter, several analysts offer a variety of approaches for reducing self-harming behavior, including the censorship of Web sites that promote radical body modification and youth-oriented prevention strategies aimed at stopping self-harm before it starts.

*"Because self-injury might have antisui-
cidal benefits, clinicians should not forbid the behavior until there are solid
replacement skills."*

Self-Injury Should Be Tolerated

Batya Swift Yasgur

*Self-mutilation should be tolerated to a certain extent because of
its anti-suicidal effects, writes Batya Swift Yasgur in the following viewpoint. Rather than viewing self-injury as an illness, clinicians should be encouraged to see it as a necessary behavior
until healthier activities can be found to replace it. Patients
should be invited to find alternatives to self-harm only when
they are ready, notes Yasgur. Yasgur is a freelance writer.*

As you read, consider the following questions:

1. In what way can self-cutting be an affirmative act, according to Caroline Kettlewell, quoted by the author?
2. According to Yasgur, what are no-harm contracts and
   what are their potential downfalls?
3. What questions can help a self-harmer determine that
   he or she is ready to stop?

Because self-injury may have antisuicidal benefits, clinicians should not forbid the behavior until there are solid replacement skills, Barent Walsh, D.S.W, said in a panel discussion at the annual meeting of the American Association of Suicidology.

Panelists at the first symposium ever convened on self injury agreed that the behavior can provide short-term relief from painful emotions, control over chaotic thoughts or experiences, and return to bodily sensations after dissociation. Individuals who engage in repeated acts of self-mutilation usually are not suicidal—they may even be avoiding suicide.

According to Caroline Kettlewell, author of *Skin Game*, cutting may be an affirmative act and a way of saying, "I bleed, therefore I am."

While there was agreement regarding the benefits of self-injury, panelists disagreed about the treatment implications of those benefits and the risk of making cessation of the behavior a condition of treatment.

Not an Illness

"I help reduce the frequency of self-injury only if that's what the patient wants. I encourage patients to see self-injury as a behavior and a choice, not an illness or psychopathology, and to use it as long as necessary until they find something better to replace it," said Dr. Tracy Alderman, Ph.D., author of *The Scarred Soul*.

Dr. Alderman's patients learn to identify triggers of self-injury and to come up with 10 alternative options, such as exercising, calling a friend, drawing with red marker on themselves, or holding an ice cube.

Dr. Alderman regards no-cutting contracts as counterproductive because they create a power struggle between therapist and patient. Patients may decide to conceal self-mutilating ac-

Cutting as a Solution

Cutting behavior awakens Katie from a disconnected emotional state to which she escapes when she is overwhelmed by despondency, anxiety, and low self-esteem. When she cuts . . . she feels focused, appropriately punished, and a bit more in control of herself. Cutting is something over which she has control.

If you discover Katie's cutting and react with horror, you will unknowingly add to her sense of shame over a behavior that is the only way she has found to relieve her emotional torment. Instead, if you notice her injuries and explain in a nonjudgmental way that you know of teenagers who try to help themselves through difficult times by cutting, she may feel a tremendous sense of relief. Explain that you're willing to help her try to understand why she has chosen cutting as a solution, and what the real problem may be.

Michael S. Jellinek, Pediatric News,
January 2005.

tivities if they are threatened with hospitalization or termination of therapy "You set them up for failure," said Dr. Alderman.

However, contracts that discourage self-injury while honoring the patient's choice to self-injure can be effective, Dr. Alderman noted. For example, the patient might agree to try two options from her list of alternatives before hurting herself.

Taking away the patient's protective mechanisms may not only increase the behavior and undermine the therapeutic relationship, but may actually be dangerous, said Dr. Walsh, executive director of the Bridge of Central Massachusetts in Northborough, Mass.

The most significant danger might be posed to those who use self-injury to deal with the hopelessness that often leads to suicide. "[I hurt myself] as a way not to kill myself," said one patient in "Women Living with Self-Injury" (Philadelphia: Temple University Press, 1999) by Jane Wegscheider Hyman, Ph.D.

Because self-injury might have antisuicidal benefits, clinicians should not forbid the behavior until there are solid replacement skills, Dr. Walsh cautioned.

A Temporary Fix

Other clinicians disagreed. "There can be no compromise where self-injury is concerned. It negatively affects all portions of a person's life, and the goal of treatment is abstinence," said Wendy Lader, Ph.D.

Self-injury is a "temporary fix," according to Dr. Lader, who is clinical director of the S.A.F.E. Alternatives Program in Berwyn, Ill. She compared self-injury to addictive behaviors, noting that alcohol rehabilitation programs do not condone the use of alcohol merely because it is the patient's coping mechanism and the patient experiences relief after taking a drink.

Participants in the S.A.F.E. Program sign a no-harm contract. Clients are taught to "sit with their painful feelings" rather than to escape through self-injury "We see this as the philosophy of empowerment—we want to speak to the healthy side of our patients," said Dr. Lader.

Because of the potential risks involved in asking patients to give up the behavior, no-harm contracts cannot be used in a vacuum but rather as part of a broader treatment protocol.

Guidelines on how to use a no-harm contract responsibly together with sample contracts, appear in *Bodily Harm: The Breakthrough Healing Program for Self-Injurers*, which is coauthored by Dr. Lader.

A Pressure-Free Approach

Different treatment strategies may be effective for different patients and may depend on the patient's reason for being in treatment, said Sarah Shaw.

Ms. Shaw reported on her study of six college students who were able to discontinue their self-injurious behavior as a result of treatment.

Patients who wished to continue self-injuring appeared to respond favorably to a pressure-free approach that gave them control of their own behavior. Patients who wanted to stop self-injuring welcomed contracts or explicit monitoring.

These alternatives seemed to provide the structure and accountability patients were seeking, said Ms. Shaw, who is a doctoral candidate in the Graduate School of Education, Harvard University, Cambridge, Mass.

> *"Are we feeding the desire for self-harm by letting those who have it in an extreme form express themselves?"*

Some Web Sites Promoting Radical Body Modification Should Be Censored

Virginia Tressider

Extreme forms of body modification such as voluntary amputation raise challenging ethical questions, notes freelance writer Virginia Tressider in the following viewpoint. While many find it disturbing that some doctors amputate healthy limbs, experts maintain that without access to safe surgical procedures, people may go on to injure themselves severely. This is particularly troublesome, given that there are "do it yourself" Web sites for people wishing to perform their own extreme body modifications. Tressider argues that such "how to" Web sites should be banned.

As you read, consider the following questions:

1. What is body dysmorphic disorder, according to Tressider?

Virginia Tressider, "Don't Try This at Home: Extreme Body Makeovers," *On Line Opinion*, April 7, 2006. Reproduced by permission.

2. According to the author, what is trepanation and why do people engage in it?

3. What does the phrase "semiotic contagion" mean?

Michael Jackson is not alone. His is merely the most famous case of excessive plastic surgery. One American woman is well on the way to realising her ambition: becoming a life-size facsimile of a Barbie doll. Another, known as "the Bride of Wildenstein" to the gossip press, had facial surgery to emphasise her cat-like features. Then she had more, followed by more. Her skin is stretched so taut that her face is both grotesque and motionless. She can no longer close her eyes.

Repellent and risible though we might think such behaviour, it would be most illiberal to think she should be prevented from disfiguring herself if she so wishes. We may wonder about surgeons who perform such operations; but, in general, a person's right to self-disfigurement is just that.

Other people want to remake themselves in other ways. Gender reassignment surgery is rather more contentious than plastic surgery, but broadly, if squeamishly, is accepted. I suspect most people, if they think about transgender surgery, tend to apply a variant of the Golden Rule, asking what they would want if they believed themselves trapped inside the wrong body. To most people, such a thing is all but incomprehensible, yet not quite beyond our capacity to imagine. Thus we are inclined towards compassion, sometimes mixed with horror and disgust.

A Question of Medical Ethics

But what of those who wish to change their bodies in other ways? Not with tattooing and exotic piercings, although this can involve far more radical modifications than most people realise, but truly arcane physical transformations.

Excessive facial surgery and gender reassignment have been categorised by some psychiatrists as a form of Body Dys-

morphic Disorder (BDD): a syndrome in which a person becomes obsessed with the ugliness of an aspect of their appearance—usually invisible to others—and will go to extraordinary
and bizarre lengths to change it. Another, less common form
is apotemnophilia: the desire to be an amputee. It is rare, but
perhaps not rare enough. And it raises serious questions of
medical ethics.

In January 2000, Scottish surgeon Robert Smith removed
healthy legs from two of his patients. This was not a tragic
surgical error: Smith described it as "the most satisfying operation I have ever performed . . . I have no doubt that what I
was doing was the correct thing for those patients".

This may seem a drastic form of patient care, but let us
consider why Smith might have thought it right. One of the
few psychiatrists with experience of apotemnophiles says:

> When a person wanting an amputation comes to a psychia-
> trist, the options are fairly limited . . . You could give them
> drugs. They're not [depressed or] psychotic so that's not go-
> ing to be any use. Counselling, psychotherapy, help them fo-
> cus on the positive things in life and get away and forget
> wanting to have an amputation.

> Unfortunately, talking treatment doesn't make a scrap of
> difference. You can talk till the cows come home. It doesn't
> make any difference. They're still going to want their ampu-
> tation.

Not just want it, but be determined to get it. The most
compelling argument for performing such surgery is the prevention of far greater harm. The cost of not amputating a
healthy limb may be greater than mere unhappiness.

In 1998 a 79-year-old man travelled to Mexico and paid
$10,000 for a black-market leg amputation. He died of gan-
grene in a motel. In 1999, a mentally competent man in Mil-
waukee severed his arm with a homemade guillotine, and
threatened to sever it again if surgeons re-attached it. A Cali-

fornian woman, refused a hospital amputation, tied her legs with tourniquets and packed them in ice, hoping gangrene would set in. She passed out and eventually gave up. Afterwards, she said she would probably have to lie under a train or blow her legs off with a shotgun.

Problematic Cases

Though rare, these cases are problematic. One reason is that we have trouble understanding why anyone would feel "incomplete" because they don't have a missing limb. The mental leap necessary to comprehend wholeness as a disability is a hard one to make.

A second is the prospect of doing something we consider monstrous to prevent something even more monstrous. The obvious precedent here is abortion. One of the more convincing arguments advanced for legalised abortion—even for those passionately against it in general—was harm minimisation: women were going to have terminations anyway, and it would be far better if they not run the risk of dying at the hands of a backyard abortionist.

There has been at least one death at the hands of a backyard amputationist, and there is no way of knowing if other apotemnophiles have died attempting somehow to do it unaided. Given the means to which many have already resorted, it is unlikely there have been no fatalities. And such people are harming, if anyone, only themselves.

A third reason is that while the treatment inspires involuntary shudders, it could be seen as merely a logical, if extreme, extension of, for example, a nose job. We accept the one, so why not the other? For the (presumably) very few who would want such surgery, it might be considered an act of mercy. And I doubt this particular operation would be the beginning of a slippery slope.

Therapeutic Amputation

The basic definition of amputation is "to cut off a projecting body part." Typically, this desire or fetish for the voluntary removal of limbs or digits is an all-consuming drive dating back to childhood. While amputation is arguably psychotic in nature, having the amputation done "cures" the problem in many cases, and the individual becomes happier and more well-adjusted. Many doctors are beginning to recognize the valid therapeutic value of amputation in a small number of cases. The desire for amputation can be similar to transsexualism, where the internal notion of self is not aligned with the external notion.

BME Encyclopedia, http://wiki.bmezine.com.

Trepanation

If, purely for argument's sake, we concede voluntary amputation might be acceptable, what should be done with another from the catalogue of unusual physical modifications—trepanation (cutting a hole in your skull)? Adherents claim this gives them a permanently higher level of spiritual vision, through increased blood volume in the capillaries of the brain. They're also willing to engage in do-it-yourself surgery when they cannot get professional medical assistance. In fact, it is possible to buy a video guide to self-trepanation.

This is, if anything, even more problematic than voluntary amputation. The claim that drilling a hole in your skull can get you to a permanently higher state of consciousness is all very well. But it is just the sort of thing that could attract someone with severe depression, or a more florid mental disorder. It also sounds like the kind of state a great many people will take a great many drugs to attempt to reach. How many of those willing to risk addiction and death for a living nirvana might think a hole in the head worth chancing? It can be done: all you need is an electric drill, and a hell of a lot of luck.

What if, unlikely though it may seem, trepanation lived up to the claims made for it? Imagine a groundswell of support building for the fashion, little by little. Where would this be most visible? Almost certainly on the Internet.

Pitfalls of the Internet

The way the Internet is being used raises, for the liberal, some truly disturbing questions. Have we unwittingly produced an effective device for disseminating mania? (A lot more worrying, I would have thought, than most varieties of pornography.) Are we feeding the desire for self-harm by letting those who have it in an extreme form express themselves?

American bioethicist Carl Elliot suggests this might be exactly what is happening. Writing on the voluntary amputation phenomenon, Elliot describes the interest shown on the Internet as "enough to support a minor industry. One discussion list has over 1,400 subscribers."

Elliot describes his interviews with apotemnophiles, for whom the 'net has proved a boon in a lot more ways than one. According to several of his contacts, it provides "instant validation." Along with instructions on how to lose your legs. But the blessing can be mixed:

To discover that she was not alone was wonderful—but it also meant that a desire she had managed to push to the back of her mind now shoved its way to the front again. It occupied her conscious thoughts in a way that was uncomfortable.

This indicates the danger inherent in exposing some things to the light. Elliot floats the idea of "semantic contagion", recounting a conversation with a professor of psychology who had been appointed to a censorship committee. Certain rather alarming sexual acts, the psychologist said, would never occur to most people in an entire lifetime of thinking about sex if they hadn't seen them pictured. In his opinion people were better off never having conceptualised such acts.

Illiberal this opinion may be, but certainly not inarguable. The idea of having one's legs amputated might never even enter the minds of some people until it is suggested to them. Yet once suggested, and paired with imagery a person's past may have primed him or her to appreciate, that act becomes possible. It has become thinkable in a way it had not been before. I think about it, therefore I can (and should) do it.

A Major Dilemma

Websites promoting these non-mainstream practices present a major dilemma for the liberal conscience. It seems abundantly clear they are promoting self-harm. One of the cornerstones of classic liberalism is that people should not be prevented from doing harmful things to themselves, so long as others are not hurt. But there are at least two questions here. The first is about empathy. Do those who deliberately maim themselves have any idea what it is like to have no choice about being, for instance, armless or not? How does the intended nirvana from trepanning compare with an intellectual disability conferred at birth? Do these people know anything about unwanted human suffering?

The second question is more difficult. Is proselytising by the converted which encourages the vulnerable to irreparably damage themselves harmful in itself—that is, precisely because it is likely to cause harm to others? While it is very tempting to think it is, along that path lies danger.

It may seem a simple matter to distinguish missionary activity on behalf of voluntary amputation from religious evangelising, for example. But what exactly is the dividing line between bliss and serenity via a hole in the head, and the same through Hare Krishna? Would a devoutly religious parent prefer her impressionable child to lose his leg or his immortal soul? The obvious answer is neither, but can we legitimately prevent people advocating a temporal harm, while continuing to allow others to try their hardest to inflict what is arguably an eternal one?

Perhaps the test case might be sites containing DIY [Do It Yourself] advice. Unlike those merely glorifying apotemno-philia, drilling a hole in your head, or just plain making your-self look ridiculous, it involves something beyond incitement. Obviously it is a test case that tries the liberal conscience hard, especially when we try to distinguish between exploiting the vulnerable and providing help to those in need. And even more so when we consider the freedom of expression given other extreme sites, such as Westboro Baptist Church, or Aryan Nations.

So do we let the amputee and trepanation sites stay, while banning "how to" sites? It can be done. It's a hard call, but when you've had the horror of seeing some of this stuff, Michael Jackson's face begins to look quite attractive.

> "Telling someone about your self-harm
> shows strength and courage. But it can
> often be a huge relief to be able to let
> go of such a secret."

Self-Injurers Should Tell Others About Their Problems

Celia Richardson

Self-injurers should be encouraged to tell others about their behavior, explains Celia Richardson in the following viewpoint. Informing others may be difficult, but it is the first step in finding the assistance they need to recover. Self-injurers are understandably reluctant to share their problems because they might receive shocked, scolding, or angry responses from friends and family, the author notes. The assurance that self-injury is usually a coping mechanism—not suicidal behavior—often helps both self-harmers and their supporters in discussions about this behavior. Richardson is director of communications at the Mental Health Foundation in London, England.

Celia Richardson, *The Truth About Self-Harm . . . For Young People and Their Friends and Families*. London: Camelot Foundation/Mental Health Foundation, 2006, pp. 16–23. © Camelot Foundation & Mental Health Foundation 2006. Reproduced by permission.

As you read, consider the following questions:

1. According to the author, what are some different ways that a self-injurer could use to tell others about their behavior?

2. What should people do when a friend or family member tells them they engage in self-harm, in Richardson's view?

3. For what reasons do self-harmers tend to continue with their behavior even after they have informed others, according to Richardson?

Should I tell someone that I am harming myself?

Yes, because this is often the first step to getting out of the cycle.

It isn't always simple or easy, and could be one of the most difficult—but most important things you do. Young people have told us that the reaction they got when they first told someone about their self-harm was very important in deciding whether or not they looked for and got further help.

While some young people have experienced negative attitudes when they have told someone, it is possible to get good support from people who understand self-harm, or who care about you and your feelings, not just the behaviour itself.

If you are worried about the person you tell sharing the information with others, you can choose to tell a health professional like a doctor or a nurse to start with, or a counsellor. You can also telephone a helpline. . . . These people have a duty to keep it to themselves while you get used to the idea of telling others. They can offer you help and advice while you prepare.

Unfortunately, some young people told us that they felt forced into discussing their self-harm, for example by teachers or health professionals who had guessed what was going on. Some young people felt very distressed by the idea that these workers would tell others—like fellow teachers or their parents. If this happens to you, you could try explaining that self-harm is a coping mechanism and not the same as suicidal behaviour.

You can ask them what will happen next, once you have told them, and who else they plan to tell or involve. You can ask them not to tell particular people. You can even ask them not to tell anyone at all, although this can be very difficult for the other person, and it can mean you do not get all of the help and support that you need.

Telling Others

What is the best way to tell someone that I have harmed myself?

It can be a very worrying decision, and it can be hard to decide who to tell and how to tell them. Telling someone about your self-harm shows strength and courage. But it can often be a huge relief to be able to let go of such a secret, or at least share it.

The most important thing of all is that you feel comfortable with who you decide to tell, what you tell them, when and where. Don't feel pressured into answering questions or saying more than you want to. You can set the pace. Remember, if you want to tell a professional or family member, you can take a friend with you to support you.

There are many ways of telling people and there are no rules about how it should be done. You can speak to someone, write to or email them, or even just show them your injuries or scars and let that pave the way to talking about it. If you tell someone in writing, think about taking some time to talk to them afterwards, as well.

It is very important, if you can, to try to focus on the feelings or situation that led you to start harming yourself, rather than on the behaviour itself. This can help people feel less bewildered about why you might be doing it.

Revealing self-harm to someone can bring out a wide range of feelings in them, both positive and negative. The person you tell may need some time to get used to what you have told them and think about their response, so try to give this to them. They may well be able to respond more positively after some time has passed and they have had the chance to think over what you have said. It can be helpful to them to know why you are telling them—whether you just want to let go of a secret you have carried on your own, or you would like their help or advice.

As hard as telling someone may be for you, it may also be very hard for the person you choose to tell—especially if it is someone close to you. They may need to get support for themselves, both before and after talking about it with you.

Try to be prepared for the fact that sometimes your situation can feel worse immediately after telling someone. But once you are over this hurdle, there is usually support available to help you recover—even if the support is through friends or family.

Seeking Help

Who can I tell?

A major factor in how the person you tell responds will be the kind of relationship they have with you, and how well they know you. A parent who might feel they are very close to you may be more shocked, for example, than a nurse.

Most people (no matter who they are, a friend, a parent, a teacher or a professional) don't really understand self-harm, and it's hard to predict how someone will react when you tell them. Try to keep in mind that they may have a range of feelings, and one of them will most likely be shock.

Young people have told us that the people they have been able to talk to included:

- Friends—young people said they were far more
  likely to talk it over with friends their own age
  than anyone else

Substitutes for Self-Harm

- using a red felt tip pen to mark where you might usually cut

- hitting a punch bag to vent anger and frustration

- hitting pillows or cushions, or having a good scream into a pillow or cushion

- rubbing ice across your skin where you might usually cut, or holding an ice-cube in the crook of your arm or leg

- getting outdoors and having a fast walk

- all other forms of exercise—these are really good at changing your mood and releasing adrenaline

- making lots of noise, either with a musical instrument or just banging on pots and pans

- writing negative feelings on a piece of paper and then ripping it up

- keeping a journal

- scribbling on a large piece of paper with a red crayon or pen

- putting elastic bands on wrists, arms or legs and flicking them instead of cutting or hitting

- calling and talking to a friend (not necessarily about self-harm)

- collage or artwork—doing something creative

- going online and looking at self-help websites

Celia Richardson, The Truth About Self-Harm, *2006.*

- Family members

- Someone at school but not necessarily a teacher you know well

- Telephone help lines were also mentioned

- Internet support: not many people had looked for help on the internet, but there are some useful sources online.

- A doctor or nurse

Some young people have said that the reaction they got when talking to health workers was unhelpful. In this case you can always seek further help. Many GPs and nurses will be sympathetic, and know how to help and no-one should be put off from seeking help because of negative attitudes.

Concern and Support

What if someone tells me they are self-harming?

The reaction a young person receives when they disclose their self-harm has a major impact on whether they go on to get help and recover. What young people who self-harm need is understanding, care and concern for their injuries, time and support as well as encouragement to talk about the underlying feelings or situations that have led them to harm themselves. Getting angry, shouting, or accusing them is likely to aggravate the situation.

Young people who have self-harmed want responses that are non-judgemental, caring and respectful. It's very important to see the person, and the reasons they have harmed themselves, and not just to focus on the harm itself. It's also important to allow the young person to take the discussion at their own pace.

Most importantly, you should try to hear about self-harm without panic, revulsion or condemnation. This can be hard as it's difficult to understand, but remember, it is quite common, and it's usually used as a way of coping by young people.

If you are a friend of the person who is self-harming, you might have some of the same reactions that a parent would—disbelief, fear for your friend, worry about what to do for the best. The person may tell you but want you to keep it a secret. This can leave you feeling distressed and isolated, with no-one to talk to yourself.

Working out what to do, or trying to decide how much danger your friend is in, is not easy. . . . It may . . . be helpful, if you are a young person, to find someone older that you trust and believe you can confide in.

Occasionally, someone may reveal to you that they have harmed themselves immediately after they have injured themselves—perhaps more than they meant to. They may be worried that they have done lasting damage. If this happens it is best to see that their injuries are attended to and they have time to recover from any physical trauma before exploring the reasons behind it.

Offering a Leading Hand

What if I discover my son or daughter or someone I care for is self-harming?

Try to be accepting and open-minded. Let the person know you are there for them, and reassure them that they are loved. Assure them that it's okay to talk about their need to self-harm, and reassure them that they have your support even if you don't understand why they are doing it or what they are going through.

Offer to lend a hand in getting them professional help; from a GP, counsellor, therapist, or community psychiatric nurse. But try to avoid taking control—many people who self-harm feel it is an important way of having some control over their lives. Try to not to take it too personally if your son or daughter cannot talk to you because you are too close.

Avoid giving ultimatums; for example, 'stop or else. . .' as they rarely work, and may well drive the behaviour underground, and you might not get any further chances to discuss the topic and really deal with it. Self-harm can be very addictive, and if a person feels the need to do it, they will normally find a way. It is important that the decision to stop comes from the person who is self-harming.

Find out more. There are a growing number of useful books on the topic of self-harm, as well as some informative websites. Educating yourself on the subject can go a long way towards helping you be understanding and supportive.

Try to sort out your own feelings. Be honest with yourself about how your daughter or son's self-harm is affecting you. It's not unusual to feel hurt, devastated, shocked, angry, sad, frightened, guilty, responsible, hopeless, or powerless. It's not easy knowing that a loved one is hurting him or herself, and it might be worth considering seeing a counsellor or therapist for yourself if you are struggling to cope with strong emotions or feel in need of support.

Remember, finding out that someone is self-harming is a real opportunity to help them deal with many other problems they are having.

Getting Assistance

What sort of help is available for young people who self-harm?

Most young people who have found help say that having someone to listen to them and help them to work on solutions to their problems and stresses is the most helpful thing of all. This is why counselling or another type of talking therapy is useful. Ask your doctor to refer you to a counsellor or psychotherapist.

Over-18's who talk to health professionals about their self-harm find that some of them are very keen to prescribe drugs such as anti-depressants. You may or may not want to try these as part of your recovery plan.

There may also be self-help groups that you can contact, where you can meet other people who have been through similar experiences to you. This can be very helpful. . . .

How can I stop harming myself?

Most importantly, try to focus on the feelings that seem to lead you to self-harm, and what is causing them. You may need the help of friends, family, a counsellor or psychotherapist, or a doctor or nurse. This is why asking for help is so important. . . .

By finding out what makes you happy, sad, angry, isolated, vulnerable or strong, you can start developing other ways of dealing with these situations and feelings. It may help just to stop and give yourself time to think them through. If you feel the need to harm yourself, give yourself a goal of getting through the next ten minutes without doing so, and try to focus on what is making you feel that way.

If you don't feel you can stop straight away, start finding other things that help you to deal with your moods and feelings. This should help you to harm yourself less and less frequently after a while—and the more effort you put in, the less strong the need to harm yourself will become.

One of the most useful things that other young people have done is to learn 'distraction methods'. These are special ways of finding a release without doing yourself any real damage. . . .

Force Does Not Work

What if I think someone is self-harming but they won't talk about it?

This can be very difficult. It is often best to discuss how the person is feeling and explain that you have noticed changes in their behaviour, rather than asking straight out. Self-harm can be a difficult subject to introduce, so take it slowly.

How do I stop someone from self-harming?

It may be very difficult if someone you care about is self-harming, but trying to force them to stop doesn't work. It is very clear that self-harm in many cases is a pattern of behaviour that may have gone on for a long time, and most young people would find it virtually impossible to give up overnight, even if they wanted to. Feeling in control is something that young people who self-harm say is very important to them. The good news is that being able to take control is one of the most important factors in the ability to recover from a pattern of self-harm, too. It is very important that the decision to stop comes from the person who is self-harming.

For many young people stopping or reducing their self-harm is a long and slow process. Young people need the opportunity to build up their coping skills gradually, and may go on harming themselves for some time.

It can take time for young people to reach the point where they can start to give up. In the meantime, learning how to cause themselves the least possible damage can be crucial, and the first step in their journey to learning other ways to deal with difficult feelings. This is called 'harm reduction' and you can find out more about this from other organisations like Siari.

For most of the young people we spoke to, the recovery process began with tackling the underlying problems that were causing their self-harm. This sometimes involved counselling, sharing their problems, or tackling bullies. Helping a young person to tackle their underlying problems is something you can very usefully do.

They also broke the habit by learning new coping strategies or using 'distraction techniques' when they felt the urge to hurt themselves. Different people need different distraction methods, and may need different things for different moods or situations. Finding what is most helpful takes time, but young people who have persisted with it emphasise that trial and error will find something that works.

"A pronounced lack of sympathy from nursing staff ... [makes] treatment in [emergency room] environments uncomfortable for [deliberate self-harmers]."

Medical Personnel Need to Respond to Self-Injurers with More Empathy

Zo Eastwick and Alec Grant

Emergency room staff need to respond to self-injurers with more sympathy, report Zo Eastwick and Alec Grant in the following viewpoint. Studies show that medical personnel often treat self-harmers as shameful time-wasters and attention-seekers and as less deserving of care than other patients, the authors point out. To rectify this problem, emergency departments should have staff on hand who have training in psychology and counseling. Emergency room workers should also undergo additional education to dispel their prejudices about self-harmers. Eastwick is manager of Aldrington House, a mental health support center in Hove, England. Grant teaches at the University of Nursing and Midwifery in Brighton, England.

Zo Ea stwick and Alec Grant, "Emotional Rescue: Deliberate Self-Harmers and A & E Departments," *Mental Health Practice*, vol. 7, no. 9, June 2004, pp. 12–15. Copyright © 2004 Royal College of Nursing Publishing Company. Reproduced by permission of the publisher and the author.

As you read, consider the following questions:

1. What is meant by the phrase "hostile-care," according to the authors?

2. According to research cited by the authors, what percentage of surveyed self-harmers expressed satisfaction with their emergency care?

3. What myths about self-harm do emergency personnel tend to believe, according to the authors?

A ccident and Emergency (A&E) departments across the UK [United Kingdom] are a frontline service, dealing with trauma in the population regardless of age or culture. Staff are required to deal with those who have encountered accidental physical injury, and address the needs of the increasing population of service users who access this service following an incident of deliberate self harm (DSH).

This paper identifies what constitutes DSH and examines the experiences of this user group attending an A&E department. It will also explore some of the pertinent literature to clarify the attitudes of professionals towards this group, and suggest some underpinning reasons why responses are often so polarised and inconsistent. Finally, specific recommendations will be made to enhance provision and bring about change in the negative attitudes of staff who regularly come into contact with such people.

What Is Deliberate Self Harm?

Deliberate self harm occurs when a person wilfully inflicts injury on him or herself without necessarily intending to commit suicide. It is often impulsive, can be undertaken in the presence of others or alone, and can sometimes be ritualistic or repetitive in its nature. Although DSH can be seen as a discrete category, distinct from attempted suicide, there is a strong relationship between people who self harm and those who eventually commit suicide. Of service users who have attended A&E departments following DSH in the preceding 12 months, 1 per cent kill themselves. Statistics also show that from 35 to 50 per cent of this total population do end their own lives. . . .

A Lack of Sympathy

A range of qualitative researchers has focused on service users' direct experiences of being treated in A&E. It has been argued that those whose behaviours are perceived as challenging tend to become labelled by staff as 'difficult patients', and users who engage in DSH fall into this category. This is confirmed in feedback from users of A&E and emergency mental health services. Service users reported feeling degraded and being treated as time wasters which, in turn, reinforced the negative feelings they held about themselves causing them to self harm in the first place.

Other studies have revealed that a pronounced lack of sympathy from nursing staff, a failure to attempt to understand their internal frame of logic for DSH, and a lack of privacy in the environment to discuss personal issues, make treatment in these environments uncomfortable for users. Smith also reported that users felt that staff saw them as a burden on the service and as failed human beings.

Harris used the term 'hostile-care' to refer to the lack of sympathy shown to women with whom she corresponded as part of her study Some of these women were told they were 'time wasting'. It appeared that by infantilising them, and appealing to their sense of shame, the women were made to feel uncomfortable and undeserving of treatment. For those who already have difficult and painful memories of, and core beliefs around, worthlessness, it is easy to see how damaging this approach can be. The women also reported instances where they had decided against recommended interventions, such as seeing a psychiatrist or requesting to be given a tetanus injection in an area other than the buttock, and had then been denied access to further treatments. This supports the position that professional attitudes are shaped by those who do not conform to the expectations, protocols or agendas of the organisation, who may be ostracised and labelled 'difficult' because of exercising their rights to choose.

Hostile Care

Hemmings reported four main areas which influence responses from nurses about service users. These were: ambivalence, judgement, punishment and the taboo nature of DSH. Examples of such treatment included: being made to wait for extended periods of time in A&E departments before being treated, the threat of either administering or withholding treatment in attempts to punish the patient, and inconsistency around treatment approaches. Hemmings speculated that such negative and punishing nursing responses relates to the possibility that DSH reminds us of our own hidden and denied self destructive urges, with users punished for breaking the rules of appropriate public performance and display.

Service users' satisfaction levels of what A&E services are able to offer may also be low. In a study of users seen by a nurse or psychiatrist in A&E, only 27 per cent expressed satisfaction with the service, and over half expressed dissatisfaction with their treatment. Service user satisfaction was higher (at 35 per cent) where they were seen by a counsellor or psychologist.

It is important to acknowledge that the type of people likely to receive treatment in A&E are those who are highly sensitised to criticism and negativity because of their own low self esteem. Most service users apparently want to be listened to, and given time to talk rather than medication. Equally, while DSH is described as a coping strategy that helps them feel more in control of themselves, users want to explore more functional ways to achieve control.

The Need for Sensitivity

Doctors in emergency rooms and urgent-care clinics should be sensitive to the needs of patients who come in to have self-inflicted wounds treated. If the patient is calm, denies suicidal intent, and has a history of self-inflicted violence, the doctor should treat the wounds as they would treat non-self inflicted injuries. Refusing to give anesthesia for stitches, making disparaging remarks, and treating the patient as an inconvenient nuisance simply further the feelings of invalidation and unworthiness the self-injurer already feels. . . . In places where people know that self-inflicted injuries are liable to lead to mistreatment and lengthy psychological evaluations, they are much less likely to seek medical attention for their wounds and thus are at a higher risk for wound infection and other complications.

Deb Martinson, "Self-Injury: Beyond the Myths," 1998–2001,
www.selfinjury.org.

How Do Professionals Respond?

To answer this question a range of literature was explored which focused on the attitudes of A&E staff from all disciplines, including those of mental health professionals, to DSH users. Common themes expressed by staff were: feeling distress, helplessness, rage, and a desire to distance themselves from this user group. Professionals acknowledged that users who engaged in DSH were viewed negatively, and often perceived as 'time-wasters' or as having an 'inadequate personality'. Some staff were described as believing that these users 'cannot be helped'—a statement which appears to allow staff to relinquish responsibility for making interventions. What underlies this picture is that staff feel that they cannot help the user, rather than that the user is beyond help.

Jeffrey and Warm identified, and robustly disputed, a range of myths that surround DSH which perpetuate unsatisfactory practice within A&E departments. These are that:

- users are merely attention seeking, and DSH is not serious since it is self inflicted.

- users who do not wish to see a psychiatrist do not wish to 'get better'.

- people who engage in DSH should be made to stop.

- self harmers are typically hysterical women under 30 years who will 'grow out of it'.

McAllister et al. argued that the inability of staff to 'cure' users is often a source of frustration. While Smith asserted that the fact that staff don't know what happens to users once they leave the department makes them feel frustrated about dealing with clients who have self harmed. Smith also suggested that the fear and anxiety held by staff about dealing with DSH comes from having no clear sense of what to do.

Concerns have been expressed by staff that they may later be vindicated in a blame culture, if the user goes on to commit suicide. Some staff acknowledged that when a person has engaged in DSH, he or she might feel more acutely desperate than someone who has been involved in an accidental injury. There seems to have been a reticence however to invest too much specifically dedicated nursing time to this group as it was perceived that this time was better spent on 'ill patients'. This suggests sublimated activity based on professionals' notions of who is more deserving of treatment. Breeze and Repper discuss how some patients become labelled 'difficult' because the dilemmas they present to staff challenge their roles, their competency and their autonomy. Labelling the patient 'difficult' thus seems to represent a projection of the perceived inability of staff to address users' needs. . . .

It is frequently reported that there is insufficient time available to address the needs of those encountering acute emotional distress, particularly in terms of sitting and talking with clients. More often, however, it is notable that the needs and agenda of those in acute distress are mismatched with the agenda of a busy A&E department located within a general hospital. Culturally and historically these places are environments associated with the immediate preservation of life, and while there is no dispute that those presenting with DSH are in need, the level of injury, and the fact that it is self inflicted, can lead staff to be dismissive.

The Need for Counseling and Training

So far, the experiences of both service users and staff who are cared for and work within the constraints of a demanding environment which is governed by political and economic agendas, and affected by cultural and historical forces, have been discussed. The question remains, though, that if service provision fails to meet the needs of, and satisfy, the user population, what changes should be made to improve this state of affairs?

The development of psychiatric liaison teams within A&E departments has gone some way to ensure that people who do present to the service are supported by workers trained to respond appropriately. These should ideally be health professionals, not necessarily psychiatrists, who are trained to carry out a full psychosocial assessment of the client's situation and needs. In response to the findings of Huband and Tantum (2002), it would seem most appropriate if these professionals had also undertaken some kind of counselling training. This relates more to the desirability of such workers to have positive attitudes and perception towards this client group, than the need to conduct therapy in A&E departments, which would of course be inappropriate.

The Need for Off-Hours Service

Where possible, this service should be made available on a 24-hour basis, or at the very least, be available 'out of hours'. People often appear to commit acts of DSH outside 'normal office hours', when day centres and community nursing services are generally closed. Services should be fast-track, become more client focused, and move away from the medical model of care. Access to non-statutory services such as self referral or short stay 'crisis-houses' would also be beneficial, rather than the only alternative to being discharged home alone being admission to acute inpatient services.

Advocate Support

Easy access to information about local and national self harm support networks needs to be made available to those attending A&E departments, as well as to those who work within the department. It would also be useful if this information is made available to relatives. Service users have also said that they would like to see more user representation in these departments in the form of 'buddies' or advocates. The option of having someone accompany the user is likely to reduce the possibility of them receiving hostile care. It may also help to foster alliance and reduce any sense of isolation, particularly if the user's desired treatment conflicts with the actual service outcomes. This type of project would naturally need to be well structured, and would require extensive service planning and collaborative working between local trusts and user groups. An action-research project looking at this type of venture could lead to an interesting evaluation of whether service user satisfaction was increased.

Staff Need Re-Education

There is a considerable amount of literature to suggest that offering education and training to staff within A&E departments goes a long way to improve current service delivery.

173

Greenwood suggests 're-educating staff to dispel prejudices', although it seems naive to believe that simply offering staff teaching sessions is going to alter longstanding and culturally reinforced beliefs about DSH.

In a small-scale study, it was identified that a series of structured teaching sessions were useful to staff. The focus was on information about DSH and what interventions might be useful, as well as how to assess accurately the risk of further DSH using a standardised tool. This resulted in staff feeling less anxious and helpless about this user group, and more confident and less irritable when dealing with them. Developing awareness of, and confidence in, the process of referral to other agencies, and bringing about increased knowledge of the legal frameworks that are in place that protect staff, were also associated with reducing the defensive attitudes of staff towards the client group.

Training and reflective peer supervision, which allows staff to open up and discuss their opinions, feelings and anxieties surrounding this client group, is possibly the most likely catalyst to shaping positive attitudes. It has also been suggested that peripheral service staff who have contact with clients who [exhibit] DSH, such as police, ambulance personnel and NHS Direct, should also have support and training of this nature.

It appears from user feedback that the main concerns of those attending A&E departments are that they receive empathic care, within a reasonable timeframe. Ideally this should be provided by someone who is interested in the user's circumstances, and able to take appropriate action in that instance or make appropriate referrals to other services that can provide support. What seems too often to stand in the way of this are negative attitudes and defensive responses of those staff who find the challenge in addressing the needs of this user groups a threat to existing custom and practice, to the power base of their profession, and autocracy of their role. This must change in order for services to improve, and we believe that through the integration of service user groups at planning level, a more effective service that meets the needs of its user population can be delivered.

"You can *get through a crisis without hurting yourself."*

Self-Help Strategies Can Reduce Self-Mutilation

Deb Martinson

In the following viewpoint, Deb Martinson details several self-help strategies that can help people reduce or stop self-injuring. She asserts that the decision to stop harming oneself should not be made hastily; sometimes it is better to simply limit the extent of self-harm and not try to stop it altogether. Her suggestions include several substitute activities, such as squeezing ice, exercising heavily, and drawing on oneself with red ink pen. Martinson is founder of the self-injury support group, Bodies Under Siege.

As you read, consider the following questions:

1. In Martinson's opinion, what statements should one be able to answer affirmatively before ceasing self-injury?
2. What is the fifteen-minute game, according to the author?
3. According to Martinson, how does one stay safe while engaging in self-injury?

Deb Martinson, "Self-Help, Organized and Otherwise," *Self-Injury: You are NOT the Only One, www.palace.net/~llama/selfinjury.* Reproduced by permission.

Deciding to stop self-injury is a very personal decision. You may have to consider it for a long time before you decide that you're ready to commit to a life without scars and bruises. Don't be discouraged if you conclude the time isn't right for you to stop yet; you can still exert more control over your self-injury [SI] by choosing when and how much you harm yourself, by setting limits for your self-harm, and by taking responsibility for it. If you choose to do this, you should take care to remain safe when harming yourself: don't share cutting implements and know basic first aid for treating your injuries.

Alderman suggests this useful checklist of things to ask yourself before you begin walking away from self-harm. It isn't necessary that you be able to answer all of the questions "yes," but the more of these things you can set up for yourself, the easier it will be to stop hurting yourself. [About the checklist, he explains:]

While it is not necessary that you meet all of these criteria before stopping SIV, the more of these statements that are true for you before you decide to stop this behavior, the better.

- I have a solid emotional support system of friends, family, and/or professionals that I can use if I feel like hurting myself.

- There are at least two people in my life that I can call if I want to hurt myself.

- I feel at least somewhat comfortable talking about SIV with three different people.

- I have a list of at least ten things I can do instead of hurting myself.

- I have a place to go if I need to leave my house so as not to hurt myself.

- I feel confident that I could get rid of all the things that I might be likely to use to hurt myself.

- I have told at least two other people that I am going to stop hurting myself.

- I am willing to feel uncomfortable, scared, and frustrated.

- I feel confident that I can endure thinking about hurting myself without having to actually do so.

- I want to stop hurting myself.

Crisis-in-the-Moment Strategies

There are several different flat-out-crisis-in-the-moment strategies typically suggested. My favorite is doing *anything* that isn't SI and produces intense sensation: squeezing ice, taking a cold bath or hot or cold shower, biting into something strongly flavored (hot peppers, ginger root, unpeeled lemon/lime/grapefruit), rubbing Ben-Gay® or Icy-Hot® or Vap-O-Rub® under your nose, sex, etc. Matching reactions and feelings is extremely useful.

These strategies work because the intense emotions that provoke SI are transient; they come and go like waves, and if you can stay upright through one, you get some breathing room before the next (and you strengthen your muscles). The more waves you tolerate without falling over, the stronger you become.

But, the question arises, aren't these things equivalent to punishing yourself by cutting or burning or hitting or whatever? The key difference is that they don't produce lasting results. If you squeeze a handful of ice until it melts or stick a couple of fingers into some ice cream for a few minutes, it'll hurt like (to quote someone I respect) "a cast-iron bitch" but it won't leave scars. It won't leave anything you'll have to explain away later. You most likely won't feel guilty after—a little foolish, maybe, and kinda proud that you weathered a crisis without SI, but not guilty.

This kind of distraction isn't intended to cure the roots of your self-injury; you can't run a marathon when you're too tired to cross the room. These techniques serve, rather, to help you get through an intense moment of badness without making things worse for yourself in the long run. They're training wheels, and they teach you that you *can* get through a crisis without hurting yourself. You will refine them, even devise more productive coping mechanisms, later, as the urge to self-injure lessens and loses the hold it has on your life. Use these interim methods to demonstrate to yourself that you can cope with distress without permanently injuring your body. Every time you do you score another point and you make SI that much less likely next time you're in crisis.

Coping Techniques

Your first task when you've decided to stop is to break the cycle, to force yourself to try new coping mechanisms. And you *do* have to force yourself to do this; it doesn't just come. You can't theorize about new coping techniques until one day they're all in place and your life is changed. You have to work, to struggle, to *make* yourself do different things. When you pick up that knife or that lighter or get ready to hit that wall, you have to make a conscious decision to do something else. At first, the something else will be a gut-level primitive, maybe even punishing thing, and that's okay—the important thing is that you made the decision, you chose to do something else. Even if you don't make that decision the next time, nothing can take away that moment of mastery, of having decided that you were not going to do it that time. If you choose to hurt yourself in the next crisis time, you will know that it is a choice, which implies the existence of alternative choices. It takes the helplessness out of the equation.

"So what *do* I do instead?" Many people try substitute activities as described above and report that sometimes they work, sometimes not. One way to increase the chances of a

Myths and Common Sense about Self-Injury	
Stereotypes about Self-Injurers	**Responses based on real experiences of self-injurers**
"It's attention-seeking."	If attention was the motivation for self-injury, it's not an efficient way of getting it. There are many easier, less painful, and less degrading ways of attracting it.
"It's a Borderline Personality Disorder."	Self-injury is not a diagnosis. What is true for one person is not necessarily true for another.
"They're manipulative."	Self-harm is a private activity. Accident and emergency departments will see only a few of the injuries before healing; it's not about its effects on others.
"Either they enjoy pain or they can't feel it."	Each person has a different pain threshold. Commonly the loss of sensation some people experience during injuring returns soon after.
"It's tension relieving."	Tension is rarely the sole pressure on an individual to injure; each person has their own pressures and triggers to injure.

distraction/substitution helping calm the urge to harm is to match what you do to how you are feeling at the moment.

First, take a few moments and look behind the urge. What are you feeling? Are you angry? Frustrated? Restless? Sad? Craving the feeling of SI? Depersonalized and unreal or numb? Unfocused?

Next, match the activity to the feeling. A few examples:

Angry, Frustrated, Restless

Try something physical and violent, something not directed at a living thing:

180

- Slash an empty plastic soda bottle or a piece of heavy cardboard or an old shirt or sock.

- Make a soft cloth doll to represent the things you are angry at. Cut and tear it instead of yourself.

- Flatten aluminum cans for recycling, seeing how fast you can go.

- Hit a punching bag.

- Use a pillow to hit a wall, pillow-fight style.

- Rip up an old newspaper or phone book.

- On a sketch or photo of yourself, mark in red ink what you want to do. Cut and tear the picture.

- Make Play-Doh or Sculpey or other clay models and cut or smash them.

- Throw ice into the bathtub or against a brick wall hard enough to shatter it.

- Break sticks.

- I've found that these things work even better if I rant at the thing I am cutting/tearing/hitting. I start out slowly, explaining why I am hurt and angry, but sometimes end up swearing and crying and yelling. It helps a lot to vent like that.

- Crank up the music and dance.

- Clean your room (or your whole house).

- Go for a walk/jog/run.

- Stomp around in heavy shoes.

- Play handball or tennis.

Sad, Soft, Melancholy, Depressed, Unhappy

Do something slow and soothing, like taking a hot bath with bath oil or bubbles, curling up under a comforter with hot cocoa and a good book, babying yourself somehow. Do whatever makes you feel taken care of and comforted. Light sweet-smelling incense. Listen to soothing music. Smooth nice body lotion into the parts or yourself you want to hurt. Call a friend and just talk about things that you like. Make a tray of special treats and tuck yourself into bed with it and watch TV or read. Visit a friend.

Craving Sensation, Feeling Depersonalized, Dissociating, Feeling Unreal

Do something that creates a sharp physical sensation:

- Squeeze ice *hard* (this really hurts). (Note: putting ice on a spot you want to burn gives you a strong painful sensation and leaves a red mark afterward, kind of like burning would.)

- Put a finger into a frozen food (like ice cream) for a minute.

- Bite into a hot pepper or chew a piece of ginger root.

- Rub liniment under your nose.

- Slap a tabletop hard.

- Snap your wrist with a rubber band.

- Take a cold bath.

- Stomp your feet on the ground.

- Focus on how it feels to breathe. Notice the way your chest and stomach move with each breath.

[NOTE: Some people report that being online while dissociating increases their sense of unreality; be cautious about logging on in a dissociative state until you know how it affects you.]

Wanting Focus

- Do a task (a computer game like tetris or minesweeper, writing a computer program, needlework, etc.) that is exacting and requires focus and concentration.

- Eat a raisin mindfully. Pick it up, noticing how it feels in your hand. Look at it carefully; see the asymmetries and think about the changes the grape went through. Roll the raisin in your fingers and notice the texture; try to describe it. Bring the raisin up to your mouth, paying attention to how it feels to move your hand that way. Smell the raisin; what does it remind you of? How does a raisin smell? Notice that you're beginning to salivate, and see how that feels. Open your mouth and put the raisin in, taking time to think about how the raisin feels to your tongue. Chew slowly, noticing how the texture and even the taste of the raisin change as you chew it. Are there little seeds or stems? How is the inside different from the outside? Finally, swallow.

- Choose an object in the room. Examine it carefully and then write as detailed a description of it as you can. Include everything: size, weight, texture, shape, color, possible uses, feel, etc.

- Choose a random object, like a paper clip, and try to list 30 different uses for it.

- Pick a subject and research it on the web.

- Try some of the games and distractions at digibeet's page; she's assembled a lot of distractions.

Wanting to See Blood

- Draw on yourself with a red felt-tip pen.

- Take a small bottle of liquid red food coloring and warm it slightly by dropping it into a cup of hot water for a few minutes. Uncap the bottle and press its tip against the place you want to cut. Draw the bottle in a cutting motion while squeezing it slightly to let the food color trickle out.

- Draw on the areas you want to cut using ice that you've made by dropping six or seven drops of red food color into each of the ice-cube tray wells.

- Paint yourself with red tempera paint.

- Get a henna tattoo kit. You put the henna on as a paste and leave it overnight; the next day you can pick it off as you would a scab and it leaves an orange-red mark behind.

Another thing that helps sometimes is the fifteen-minute game. Tell yourself that if you still want to harm yourself in 15 minutes, you can. When the time is up, see if you can go another 15. I've been able to get through a whole night that way before.

If Nothing Seems to Work

Sometimes you will make a good-faith effort to keep from harming yourself but nothing seems to work. You've slashed a bottle, your hand is numb from the ice, and the urge is still twisting you into knots. You feel that if you don't harm yourself, you'll explode. What now?

Get out the questions Kharre asks. It's a good idea to have several copies of these printed out and ready to use. . . .

Answer these as honestly and in as much detail as you are able to right now. No one is going to see the answers except you, and lying to yourself is pretty pointless. If, in all honesty, you see no other answer to #8 but yes, then give yourself permission, but set definite limits. Do not allow the urge to control you; if you choose to give in to it, then choose it. Decide beforehand exactly what you will allow yourself to do and how much is enough, and stick to those limits. Keep yourself as safe as you can while injuring yourself, and take responsibility for the injury.

The questions:

1. Why do I feel I need to hurt myself? What has brought me to this point?
2. Have I been here before? What did I do to deal with it? How did I feel then?
3. What I have done to ease this discomfort so far? What else can I do that won't hurt me?
4. How do I feel right now?
5. How will I feel when I am hurting myself?
6. How will I feel after hurting myself? How will I feel tomorrow morning?
7. Can I avoid this stressor, or deal with it better in the future?
8. Do I need to hurt myself?

Staying Safe

A few things to keep in mind should you decide that you do need to hurt yourself:

- Don't share cutting implements with anyone; you can get the same diseases (hepatitis, AIDS, etc.) addicts get from sharing needles.

- Try to keep cuts shallow. Keep first aid supplies on hand and know what to do in the case of emergencies.

- Do only the minimum required to ease your distress. Set limits. Decide how much you are going to allow yourself to do (how many cuts/burns/bruises, how deep/severe, how long you will allow yourself to engage in SI), keep within those boundaries, and clean up and bandage yourself later. If you can manage that much, then at least you will be exerting some control over your SI.

> *"Effective prevention (and treatment) approaches will include a focus on enhancing individuals' capacity to cope with adversity."*

Prevention Strategies Should Be Adopted

Cornell University Family Life Development Center

The following viewpoint is excerpted from a research report drafted by the Cornell University Family Life Development Center. The report details effective ways to detect, intervene in, and prevent self-injurious behavior among teenagers. Researchers believe that teaching individuals non-harmful ways of coping with stress is necessary for both treatment and prevention. In addition, fostering social connectedness and healthy communication would enable more youths to reach out to others when they are feeling emotionally burdened. Educating young people about the influence of media and environmental stresses may help them to avoid dangerous coping strategies.

As you read, consider the following questions:

1. What are some of the signs that an individual may be engaging in self-injurious behavior, according to the authors?

"What Do We Know About Self-Injury?" *Cornell Research Program on Self-Injurious Behavior in Adolescents and Young Adults, www.crpsib.com.*, Reproduced by permission.

2. Why might "single-shot" educational approaches to preventing self-injury backfire, in the authors' opinion?

3. Why do the authors believe that targeting environmental sources of stress may be a more effective prevention strategy than targeting youths who may be at risk for self-harming behavior?

Detecting and intervening in self-injurious behavior can be difficult since the practice is often secretive and involves body parts which are relatively easy to hide. Although experienced therapists in this area can offer advice based on experience, few studies which actually test detection, intervention and treatment strategies have been conducted. The suggestions which follow are those which evolve naturally from existing literature and from interviews with practitioners with significant experience in self-injurious behavior.

- *Unexplained burns, cuts, scars, or other clusters of similar markings on the skin can be signs of self-injurious behavior.* Arms, fists, and forearms opposite the dominant hand are common areas for injury. However, evidence of self-injurious acts can and do appear on pretty much every body part possible. Other signs include: inappropriate dress for season (consistently wearing long sleeves or pants in summer), constant use of wrist bands / coverings, unwillingness to participate in events / activities which require less body coverage (such as swimming or gym class), frequent bandages, odd / unexplainable paraphernalia (e.g. razor blades or other implements which could be used to cut or pound), and heightened signs of depression or anxiety. When asked, individuals who self-injure may offer stories which seem implausible or which may explain one, but not all, physical indicators such as "It happened while I was playing with my kitten." It is important that questions about the marks be non-threatening and emotionally neutral. Evasive responses are common. Not knowing how to broach the subject is often what restrains concerned individuals from probing. However, concern for their well-being is often what many who self-injure most need and persistent but neutral probing may eventually elicit honest responses.

- *Schools, parents, medical practitioners, and other youth-serving professionals all have an important role to play in identifying self-injury and in assisting youth in getting help.* Unfortunately, lack of information on self-injury has hampered the creation of informational materials and/or treatment options. The S.A.F.E. Alternatives program in the Linden Oaks Hospital in Edward, Illinois is one of the only existing inpatient treatment programs specific to self-injury in the nation (see www.selfinjury.com). Moreover, while a small but growing body of evidence exists to assist those helping individual self-injurers, little literature exists to explain and address the environmental factors that contribute to adoption of the practice. For those who encounter self-injurious adolescents, creating a safe environment is critical. This can be difficult with youth who have suffered trauma or abuse. Drawing from a number of studies in this area, Kress, Gibon and Reynods (2004) maintain that structure, consistency, and predictability are important elements in forming relationships with self-injurious youth. Developing plans which emphasize a) taking responsibility for the behavior, b) reducing the harm inflicted by the behavior, c) identifying and more positively reacting to self-injury triggers and physical cues, d) identifying safe people and places for assistance when needing to reduce the urge to self-injure, and e) avoiding objects which could be used to self-injure (e.g., paper clips, staples, erasers, sharp objects) can help to reduce the harm associated with self-injurious practices and establish trust. This plan should serve to help stabilize the student and to provide structure and support until community-based counseling can begin.

The Need to Avoid Shaming Responses

- *Avoid displaying shock, engaging in shaming responses, or showing great pity.* The intensely private and shameful feelings associated with self-injury prevent many from seeking treatment. Self-injurers often appear in emergency rooms only when self-inflicted wounds are so severe that they require medical treatment such as stitches or bone-setting. Because so little is known about self-injury, it is often misunderstood by medical staff members who provide the initial treatment. This misunderstanding may lead to extremely inappropriate treatment, such as stitching without anesthetic or intense feelings of frustration for the provider who asks, "Why is this person hurting *him or herself?*" Such reactions, if expressed in shocked or punitive ways, may reinforce the self-injurious behavior and its underlying causes and encourage the self-injurer not to seek care in the future. Self-injury is most often a silent, hidden practice aimed at either squelching negative feelings or overcoming emotional numbness. Being willing to listen to the self-injurer while reserving shock or judgment encourages them to use their voice, rather than their body, as a means of self-expression.

Preventing Self-Harm

Preventing self-injury involves identifying people who are most at risk and then offering help. For instance, those at risk can be taught healthy coping skills that they can then draw upon during periods of intense distress. But identifying those at risk isn't always easy.

If you have a loved one who seems to have signs or symptoms of depression or who seems overwhelmed by events in his or her life, early intervention, such as psychotherapy, may prevent a worsening of problems that can lead to self-injury. . . .

If you are contemplating self-injury for the first time, turn instead to a trusted friend or loved one, or a medical professional. They can help you find better options—options that won't leave you permanently scarred.

Mayo Clinic, "Self-Injury/Cutting," August 3, 2006,
www.mayoclinic.com.

- *Self-injury is, most often, not a suicidal gesture.* It is important to differentiate between a self-injurious act and a suicide attempt at the outset since the two require different treatments. Mental health and counseling resources should be provided since self-injury is often a signal of underlying, unresolved distress. More long-term treatments may involve psychiatric and/or medical therapy.

- *Self-injury serves a function—explicitly teaching more appropriate coping strategies may be one way to provide self-injurers with adaptive alternatives.* Self-injury is most common in youth having trouble coping with anxiety. An important part of treatment is helping youth to find other, more positive ways to accomplish the same psychological and emotional outcome, i.e., explicitly teach coping skills. It is thus important to focus on skill building in individual youth, and to identify and remedy the environmental stressors that trigger self-injury. It is important to substitute a more positive coping strategy and not just eliminate the self-injury, as another self-destructive behavior, such as drug abuse, may take its place. Drug therapy may help in some cases as well. Some patients using prescribed drugs for depression have found a reduction in the urge to self-injure while taking these medications. Therapy may be useful in exploring the underlying causes of self-injury. A combination of the above treatments may significantly reduce or completely eliminate self-injurious behavior. . . .

Self-Injury Among Groups

- *Assess level of group involvement.* Anecdotal evidence of self-injurious practices among groups of youth is increasingly common. Group self-injury is often a means of group bonding and membership and, as such, is undertaken with aims other than reducing anxiety or coping with overwhelming negative feeling—motivations strongly associated with "lone" self-injurious practices. These differences in motivation are likely to necessitate differences in approaches to intervention and prevention. However, because there also is evidence that self-injurious behavior can be contagious in institutional settings and anecdotal evidence that it is also showing contagious tendencies in school settings, identifying and intervening in group self-injurious activities is important. The possibility for serious unintentional injury or infection to occur and / or for individuals who begin to self-injure as a means of group membership to develop a dependency on the practice over time augments the importance of early intervention and prevention. Identifying who is involved, the nature and lethality of the self-injurious activities used, and the purpose served for individuals and the groups constitute important first steps in effective detection and intervention. . . .

Prevention

Virtually nothing has been written on effective ways of preventing the adopting of self-injurious practices. Indeed, this is an area badly in need of research. However, we can begin to craft possible strategies by acknowledging dominant reasons for initiating and maintaining self-injurious practices and from lessons in related fields, such as disordered eating.

- *Enhance capacity to cope.* Inability to find alternate satisfying ways of coping with strong negative feelings is a highly consistent motivation for engaging in self-injury. Indeed, one of the most common reasons for ceasing the behavior given in our recent student survey is the adoption of other coping mechanisms. It thus seems logical that effective prevention (and treatment) approaches will include a focus on enhancing individuals' capacity to cope with adversity. Indeed, this focus is one of the elements of Dialectical Behavior Therapy (DBT)—one of the more common and effective treatment approaches used with self-injurious behavior. Broad agreement among mental health professionals that capacity to cope is declining in the general population of adolescent and young adults suggests that enhancing capacity to cope may also be a useful part of universal and targeted prevention approaches. Building on existing strengths and exploiting opportunities within institutional curriculum to help youth explore diverse methods of coping with negative feelings may help accomplish this objective.

- *Enhance social connectedness.* Those who practice self-injurious behavior also report high levels of perceived loneliness, less dense social networks, less affectionate relationships with their parents, and a history of emotional and/or sexual abuse. They are also more likely to suffer from diminished self-esteem, feelings of invisibility, and shame. Indeed, feeling invisible and inauthentic are common themes among self-injurious students we have interviewed for our studies. Approaches in which adolescents and adults are aided in recognizing and building on existing strengths, in reaching out to and connecting way with others in an authentic and meaningful way, and in participating in activities which allow them to feel meaningfully linked to something larger than themselves may help to shape a more positive view of the self. This may ultimately lessen reliance on potentially damaging coping mechanisms.

- *Avoid strategies aimed primarily at raising knowledge of forms and practices.* Strategies aimed primarily at raising knowledge generally use single-shot or knowledge enhancement approaches to educate universal or targeted groups of youth about specific risk behaviors, practices, forms and consequences. In their review of eating disorder prevention strategies and research Levine and Smolak summarize research which suggests that single-shot awareness raising strategies (e.g., educational assemblies or workshops) are, at best, either not effective or only effective in raising short term knowledge and are, at worst, linked to increases in the behavior they intend to stop. Adverse effects were particularly evidenced in high school and college populations. Repeated and rigorous evaluation of the popular DARE program aimed at reducing drug use among youth has also been shown to be ineffective and, at worst, harmful. In many ways, these findings are consistent with common sense when regarded in the context of developmental processes—adult attention to specific risk behaviors, particularly if highly informative but of short duration or thoughtful follow-up, can be scintillating to adolescents interested in seeking adult attention or taking risks. Strategies which raise awareness about underlying factors (e.g. role of media or the cultural thinness ideal in promoting eating disorders) are *not* the same as those which simply educate about the prevalence, forms and practices associated with a specific issue and are likely to be more effective in positively raising awareness.

Recognizing Self-Harming Behavior

- *Equip staff and faculty to recognize and respond to signs of self-injurious behavior.* Although it may be unwise to share detailed information about self-injurious behavior with large groups of youth, adults likely to encounter adolescents or young adults who engage is self-injurious behavior do need to know signs and symptoms. They also need to know what to do if they suspect or know someone is using self-injurious practices. Toward this end, raising awareness among adults as well as establishing protocols for referral is helpful for those who work directly with youth.

- *Focus on increasing staff and student capacity to recognize distress.* As with many risk behaviors, our research shows that peers are most often the first to know or suspect that a friend is using self-injurious practices. As such, peers constitute the "front line" in detection and intervention. In light of the above recommendation to avoid awareness raising strategies about self-injurious behaviors with youth, we advocate concentrating effort on assisting young people to recognize *general symptoms of distress* in their peers. Self-injurious behavior could be one of several categories of behaviors and perceptions assessed (mixing both positive and negative indicators avoids a soley deficit-based slant to findings) such as perceived wellbeing, eating disorders, life satisfaction, depression, relationships with adults, suicidality, etc. Additionally, while a few examples might be useful in explaining what is meant by self-injury, detailed description of forms could be avoided. In addition to educating about how to recognize distress, students could be encouraged to seek assistance and coached on specific strategies for getting help.

Encouraging Help-Seeking

- *Promote and advertise positive norms related to help-seeking and communication about mental and emotional status and needs.* It often requires more than a program or two to change embedded patterns. The tendency for peers to show loyalty to friends rather than to adults is strong (and, in many ways, fundamentally socially adaptive). Peers with knowledge of a friend's dangerous behavior may be unlikely to share that knowledge with an adult without concentrated effort by adults to alter adolescent *and* adult norms about help-seeking and communication—particularly communication between adolescents and adults. Strategies focused on altering community norms in social support and help-seeking have been shown to be exceptionally effective in suicide prevention in a general population of adults in the US Air Force. Whether this approach will prove effective with self-injurious and suicide-related behaviors in adolescent and young adult populations is the subject of current research. . . .

Addressing Risk Factors

- *Address sources of stress in external environment.* The relationship between the sheer volume of stress or risk factors individuals confront and negative outcomes is well documented. Researchers have overwhelmingly shown that the more risk factors an individual confronts, the less like they are to thrive and the more likely they are to exhibit negative behaviors and attitudes. The capacity to manage multiple stressors simultaneously is particularly difficult for children and adolescents who [are] attempting to successfully meet core developmental needs as well. Although empirically impossible to verify, the argument that contemporary children and youth confront an increasingly complex and varied set of stress and risk factors when compared to previous generations is persuasive and may be one reason for increases in rates of mental illness, including self-injurious behavior. If so, as Levine and Smolak argue for eating disorders, targeting environmental sources of stress may be a fundamentally more effective prevention strategy than targeting individual youth deemed to be at risk for self-injurious or other concerning behaviors.

- *Educate youth to understand the role media plays in influencing behavior.* Media has consistently been shown to affect child and adolescent behavior in profound ways. Examination of the possible role media plays in spreading the idea of self-injurious behavior is one of the projects undertaken as part of this study program. Our preliminary findings support the assumption that images, songs, and news articles in which self-injurious behavior is featured has increased significantly over the past decade. As Brumberg has argued for eating disorders, highly visible public displays of self-injurious behavior may add potentially lethal behaviors to the repertoire of young people exploring identity options. Helping adolescents and young adults become critical consumers of media may lessen their vulnerability to adoption of glamorized but fundamentally poor coping strategies.

> "Western beauty practices from make-up
> to labiaplasty ... should be included
> within UN understandings [of harmful
> cultural / traditional practices]."

Western Beauty Customs Should Be Defined as Harmful Cultural Practices

Sheila Jeffreys

Socially approved beauty practices such as breast implants and tummy tucks should be included in the United Nations definition of harmful cultural and traditional practices, argues Sheila Jeffreys in the following viewpoint. These unnecessary surgeries are seriously invasive and often cause pain and distress in women, Jeffreys points out. The fashion, beauty, and entertainment industries should be held accountable for encouraging this form of self-mutilation, she concludes. Jeffreys is a researcher and lecturer at the University of Melbourne. This viewpoint is excerpted from her book Beauty and Misogyny: Harmful Cultural Practices in the West.

Sheila Jeffreys, "Beauty and Misogyny," *Arena Magazine*, vol. 78, August–September 2005, pp. 46–49. Copyright 2005 Arena Printing and Publications Pty. Ltd. Reproduced by permission.

As you read, consider the following questions:

1. When did cosmetic surgery begin in the United States, according to Jeffreys?
2. According to a *Glamour* magazine survey, what percentage of men would encourage their wife or girlfriend to get breast implants if it were safe, free, and painless?
3. What other kinds of mutilation are spawned by the entertainment industry, in the author's opinion?

According to United Nations documents such as the 'Fact Sheet on Harmful Traditional Practices', harmful cultural/traditional practices are understood to be damaging to the health of women and girls, to be performed for men's benefit, to create stereotyped roles for the sexes and to be justified by tradition. This concept provides a good lens through which to examine practices that are harmful to women in the west—such as beauty practices. But western practices have not been included in the definition or understood in international feminist politics as harmful in these ways. Indeed there is a pronounced western bias in the selection of practices to fit the category such that only one western practice, violence against women, is included. The implication is that western cultures do not have harmful practices such as female genital mutilation that should cause concern. I argue that western beauty practices from make-up to labiaplasty do fit the criteria and should be included within UN understandings. The great usefulness of this approach is that it does not depend on notions of individual choice; it recognises that the attitudes that underlie harmful cultural practices have coercive power and that they can and should be changed.

Socially Approved Self-Injury

Changing attitudes and practices will not be easy, however, particularly given the normalisation of cosmetic surgery. For example, according to Elizabeth Haiken in her book *Venus*

Envy, between 1982 and 1992, the percentage of people in the US who approved of cosmetic surgery increased by 50 per cent and the percentage who disapproved decreased by 66 per cent. Cosmetic surgery, she says, began at the same time in the US as the phenomenon of beauty pageants and the development of the beauty industry in the 1920s. Haiken points out that cosmetic surgery can be seen as an indication of the failure of feminist attempts to dismantle male domination: 'Cosmetic surgery', she argues, 'has remained a growth industry because, in greater numbers, American women gave up on shaping that entity called "society" and instead turned to the scalpel as the most sensible, effective response to the physical manifestations of age'. Cosmetic surgery, as Haiken points out, was always about putting women into the beauty norms of a sexist and racist society. Women who did not fit American norms had to cut up. Thus by the mid-century, 'Jewish and Italian teenage girls were getting nose jobs as high school graduation presents'.

Breast augmentation, however, is more recent than other types of cosmetic surgery and dates from the early 1960s. This places its origins in the so-called sexual revolution in which men's practice of buying women in prostitution was destigmatised through the ideology of sexual liberalism. The sex industry expanded swiftly in the US through pornography and stripping. Breast augmentation was associated in the beginning with 'topless dancers and Las Vegas showgirls'. The method of enlarging breasts for men's pornographic delight in this early period was silicone injections rather than implants. Strippers, Haiken tells us, were getting a pint of silicone injected into each breast through weekly injections. The origin of the practice lay in the prostitution industry created in postwar Japan to service US soldiers who found Japanese women too small for their taste: 'Japanese cosmetologists pioneered the use of silicone ... after such solutions as goats' milk and paraffin were found wanting'.

A Harmful Cultural Practice

The effects on the health of victims of this harmful cultural practice were very severe. The silicone 'tended to migrate'. It could turn up in lymph nodes and other parts of the body, or form lumps that would mask the detection of cancer. As Haiken comments: 'At worst, then, silicone injections could result in amputation, and at the very least all recipients were expected to have "pendulous breasts" by the time they were forty'. In 1975 it was reported that 'surgeons suspected that more than twelve thousand women had received silicone injections in Las Vegas alone; more than a hundred women a year were seeking help for conditions ranging from discoloration to gangrene that developed anywhere from one to fourteen years later'. Silicone implants replaced injections but concerns about the health effects caused the American Food and Drug Administration to impose an almost total ban in April 1992. Women who received implants regularly lost sensation in their nipples after the surgery and suffered problems such as encapsulation when scar tissue rendered the breasts hard. Saline implants were favoured where silicone was outlawed. Nonetheless, by 1995, when *Glamour* magazine asked men, 'If it were painless, safe, and free, would you encourage your wife or girlfriend to get breast implants?' 55 per cent said yes. This figure does indicate where the pressure for women to have implants originates.

One impulse that underlies women's pursuit of breast implant surgery may be depression. Several studies have shown that there is an unusually high suicide rate among those who have implants. A 2003 Finnish study found that the rate was three times higher than among the general population. There is controversy as to the reason for this high rate. Some researchers say it indicates that women who have implants are already depressed and have a tendency towards suicide. The high rate would then suggest that the surgery does not cure the depression. Others say that the suicides may relate to the

Surgical Abuse

We've all seen haunting examples of what can happen when people with distorted self-images and plenty of money meet up with a doctor who's willing to cater to them. "If you keep looking long enough, you can always find someone who will do anything to you," says Helen Colen, MD, a plastic surgeon in private practice in Manhattan. "People from all kinds of other specialties are going into plastic surgery because it's profitable. Doctors have tremendous power, and some of them abuse it for financial gain." These are the surgeons who are likely to push a series of procedures you never considered, and are responsible for such sideshow alterations as quadruple-D breast implants, calf and buttock implants, repeated nose jobs, "labia lifts," (yes, they're exactly what you'd imagine), risky "hand rejuvenation," and toe shortening.

"Extreme Beauty," O, The Oprah Magazine, *August 2003.*

degree of pain and anxiety women suffer because of the implants. Either way, the suicide rate suggests that breast implants are not positively correlated with women's mental health.

Plastic Surgery Message Boards

The routinisation of seriously invasive cosmetic surgery is evident in the discussion fora and message boards the industry has set up in recent years to gain clients and encourage women to pay for their services. The message boards are sections of the websites of cosmetic surgery clinics and referral services. They are interesting because they demonstrate how forms of interaction that women have developed to deal with oppression—gossip, sharing of experiences, encouragement and support—have been exploited to increase industry profits. The discussions resemble a distorted form of consciousness-raising techniques. Women discuss their pain and distress but instead of criticising the process of exploitation in which they have been involved, they support each other in going through with surgery and getting more. The boards are a consciousness-lowering medium.

One exchange on the Plastic Surgery Message Board in June 2004 gives an impression of how serious the sequelae can be. Tenta writes that she had a tummy tuck four years ago, which 'involved major complications'. She had to go to hospital to have the 'binder' cut off. She says: "At the time I had pubic area swelling and was told that it would go away. It has been 4 years and my pubic area still is swollen. I feel very uncomfortable and can't wear tights and usually purchase pants/skirts one size bigger."

Danya replies that liposuction would probably solve the problem and explains that the mons pubis sometimes after a tummy tuck "gets pulled up because of the tension from having a nice flat tummy".

Other problems that women discuss include swelling, bruising, pain, numbness, itching, smell, unwanted lumps, dents and constipation. One woman, Calimom, complains on the Implantinfo Support Forum about pain: "My PS [plastic surgeon] has me massaging for 2-3 minutes every hour but today it really hurts. I'm very bruised and swollen below my breasts and it's starting to really burn there when I massage. Should I continue but just be gentler?"

On the same message board another woman, Emily, talks of the problems she has four days after both liposuction and implants in her breasts: "I was not expecting it to be this bad. Where my PS sucked out tissue on the side is just so painful. I just want to be able to wash my own hair, feed myself, and go to the bathroom alone ... when should I really start feeling back to normal with pretty good usage of my arms? I don't know if I'll make it much longer!"

The surgery these women have had is the everyday practice of modern cosmetic surgeons. The message boards demonstrate the extent to which such surgery can now be the aspiration even of young teenage girls. A labiaplasty message board attached to lasertreatments.com has a message from a fourteen-year-old girl so desperate to have surgery on her labia and mons pubis that she has considered cutting up her own body: "Hi I'm 14 and I've been wanting labiaplasty too. (and lol I've gotten so mad I thought about taken the knife myself too!) It's bothered me for as long as I can remember and as much as guys say it's a turn-on I still hate it . . . I was also looking into getting liposuction of the mons pubis . . . and I know it seems weird to get liposuction there but I'm skinny but then fat there and it bothers me so much."

Fortunately a woman responded to her, telling her that it is normal for young girls of her age to be concerned about the way their body is developing and she should not consider altering it until she is fully grown. . . .

Midriff Mutilation

The body types featured in sexual entertainment spawn other forms of extreme mutilation of women. The hipster pants fashion, particularly as portrayed by Britney Spears, has led to a surge in lipo-surgery to create Britney-style flat stomachs. [The Australian magazine] NW features a woman who undertook the nine-hour operation, costing thousands of dollars, because she was 'so embarrassed by her belly'. The patient, Hilary Coritore, explains: "I'd just like to feel proud of my figure, but right now I'm so ashamed of my belly—it just hangs there. Britney Spears has an amazing stomach, and I'd give anything to look like that. She wears all those low pants and I just wish I could have a stomach as flat as hers."

In the operation, she receives liposuction to her thighs and upper abdomen to help 'show off the tummy tuck that took place as follows: 'A large 15cm-square slice of Hilary's belly is then cut off and thrown away. The whole area from Hilary's pubic bone up to her navel has been removed'. She received breast implants at the same time to utilise the same incision. Cosmetic surgeons like to give the impression that they perform these mutilations for the sake of the women rather than to exploit women's low self-esteem to line their pockets. The surgeon in Coritore's operation says that 'all my girls' in the compulsory 'before' photograph of their almost naked bodies look 'shy, timid and insecure', but, 'the change I see in my patients in just a few days is so amazing'.

Feasts for Men's Eyes

Cosmetic surgeons seem to like to surgically construct their wives, as advertisements for their business, and, presumably, because they then have their favoured fetish objects easily available in their homes. One such [surgeon] is Ox Bismarchi who, according to NW, cut up his wife, Brazilian model Angela Bismarchi, ten times in two years. He encouraged her to undertake more surgery and carried it out himself. He says: 'When I look at her, I see my own creation'. He is twenty-five years older than his twenty-eight-year-old wife. He gave her 'Pamela Anderson-like breasts, a tiny waist and a totally flat stomach' as well as placing 'non-absorbent gels' in his wife's 'calves, lips and cheeks'. He even gave her a dimple in her chin.

The cosmetic surgery carried out on women in the mainstream entertainment industry is directed towards making them conform to men's sexual fantasies in order to earn their subsistence. In extreme forms women are made into freaks who cannot physically support the weight of their own breasts and whose faces are contorted masks, but the purpose is related to the dictates of the sexual corvee. The women are mutilated to provide feasts for men's eyes.

Cosmetic Surgery Is Mutilation

The forms of mutilation that are socially approved because they make women more sexually attractive to men—cosmetic surgery and some forms of piercing and tattooing—are usually separated out from the wave of self-mutilations of more extreme or unusual varieties involved in body modification. It is not clear to me that they should be, however. The seriously invasive surgery involved in breast implantation, for instance, would be considered savage if it was carried out at a body modification convention. When it is done by surgeons in the name of relieving the supposedly ordinary distress of women about their appearance it can be seen as unremarkable. The connection between amputee identity disorder and cosmetic surgery is usefully made by Dan Edelman who asks: 'When in both cases the language used implies a sense of Otherness with respect to one's body, wherein lies the difference in the decision to remove a "foreign" limb versus tucking the tummy or lifting the face of a body that is not a "home"?'

In the face of an epidemic in the west of increasingly severe forms of self-mutilation, it may be time to ask how the attacks on the body may be stopped. The fashion, beauty, pornography and medical industries that justify and promote these forms of self-harm are parasitic on the damage male-dominant western societies enact on women and girls and vulnerable constituencies of boys and men.

Periodical Bibliography

The following articles have been selected to supplement the diverse views presented in this chapter.

| Lynette Arbuthnot and Mark Gillespie | "Self Harm: Reviewing Psychological Assessment in Emergency Departments," *Emergency Nurse*, March 2005. |

Sidhartha Hakim and Saeed Nazir — "How to Deal with Children Who Self-Harm," *GP*, September 24, 2004.

Michael S. Jellinek — "Cutting' Pain More than Skin Deep," *Pediatric News*, January 2005.

Barbara Krantowitz — "Brush with Perfection," *Newsweek*, October 30, 2006.

Robert T. London — "Trichotillomania: Finding Solutions," *Clinical Psychiatry News*, September 2004.

Phillip Olson — "Scar: An Essay," *La Crosse Tribune*, June 10, 2006.

O, The Oprah Magazine — "Extreme Beauty," August 2003.

Dina Roth Port — "'I Couldn't Stop Pulling Out My Hair,'" *Cosmopolitan*, February 2003.

Anabel Unity Sale — "Dealing with the Hurt," *Community Care*, December 13, 2001.

Martin Smith — "Avoiding Harm," *Young Minds Magazine*, November–December 2004.

Judy Specht, Adam J. Singer, and Mark C. Henry — "Self-Inflicted Injuries in Adolescents Presenting to a Suburban Emergency Department," *Journal of Forensic Nursing*, Spring 2005.

Nancy Walsh — "Stemming the Tide of Self-Cutting in Adolescents," *Clinical Psychiatry News*, May 2002.

For Further Discussion

Chapter 1

1. Most of the contributors in this volume maintain that self-mutilation is a serious problem and that self-injurers need to learn alternative ways of coping with emotional difficulties. Yet Alex Williams insists that *avoiding* the urge to self-injure can be more harmful than self-injury itself. Why was this true in her case? Does her background as a volunteer with mental health problems lend credence to her argument? Why or why not?

2. Self-mutilation is commonly thought to be a problem limited to teenage girls and young women. But the viewpoint by LifeSIGNS argues otherwise. According to LifeSIGNS, why do many people still think that self-injury is a female issue? How does this perception affect male self-injurers? Use evidence from the text to support your answer.

Chapter 2

1. Both Sheila Jeffreys and Melanie Phillips contend that self-mutilation includes body modification (such as body piercing, tattooing, and certain kinds of cosmetic surgery) and should be opposed. Kathlyn Gay, Christine Whittington, and Debbie Jefkin-Elnekave, however, maintain that body modification is often a form of artistic self-expression or a marker of cultural identity. Which of these arguments do you find to be more persuasive? Why?

2. After reading Pippa Wysong's viewpoint, are you more or less likely to encourage a friend to get a body piercing or a tattoo? Explain.

3. Virginia L. Blum argues that cosmetic surgery can be a self-mutilating act—particularly when women have sur-

gery to relieve themselves of anguish about their appearance. Conversely, Michelle Copeland sees cosmetic surgery as a way to boost self-esteem and improve one's mental health. What kinds of support does each author use to back up her argument? Whose argument is more convincing, in your opinion?

Chapter 3

1. Kimberly Sevcik uses anecdotes, narrative, and descriptive details to help support her argument about the relationship between cultural oppression and self-mutilation among women in Afghanistan. Cathy Fillmore, Colleen Anne Dell, and Elizabeth Fry cite studies and survey research to back up their conclusions about the connection between domestic abuse and female self-injury. Which strategy do you find more compelling? Why?

Chapter 4

1. Why do the clinicians featured in Batya Swift Yasgur's viewpoint argue that self-injury should be tolerated? Do you agree with the statement that "self-injury [is] a behavior and a choice, not an illness or psychopathology"? Defend your answer using evidence from the text.

2. In her viewpoint, Virginia Tressider argues that some—but not all—Web sites that promote extreme forms of body modification should be censored. What particular kind of Web sites need to be shut down, in her opinion? Why does she refrain from advocating the banning of all body modification Web sites?

3. The viewpoints in this chapter include several recommendations for reducing self-injurious behavior. Consider each recommendation and then list some arguments for and against each one. Note whether the arguments are based

on facts, values, emotions, or other considerations. If you believe a recommendation should not be considered at all, explain why.

Organizations to Contact

The editors have compiled the following list of organizations concerned with the issues debated in this book. The descriptions are derived from materials provided by the organizations. All have publications or information available for interested readers. The list was compiled on the date of publication of the present volume; the information provided here may change. Be aware that many organizations take several weeks or longer to respond to inquiries, so allow as much time as possible.

Alliance of Professional Tattooists, Inc. (APT)
9210 S. Highway 17-92, Maitland, FL   32751
(407) 831-5549
e-mail: info@safe-tattoos.com
Web site: www.safe-tattoos.com

The Alliance of Professional Tattooists is a nonprofit educational organization that was founded in 1992 to address the health and safety issues facing the tattoo industry. The organization seeks to dispel myths and misconceptions surrounding tattooing through education and awareness and holds seminars on disease prevention at tattoo conventions across the United States. APT publishes several pamphlets, including *Basic Guidelines for Getting a Tattoo*, *So You Want to Be a Tattoo Artist*, and *The First Step in Safe Tattooing*

American Association of Plastic Surgeons (AAPS)
900 Cummings Center, Suite 22 1-U, Beverly, MA   01915
(978) 927-8330 • fax: (978) 524-8890
Web site: www.aaps1921.org

Established in 1921, the AAPS is dedicated to advancing the science and art of plastic surgery through education, research, scientific presentations, and professional interaction. The organization publishes the *AAPS Newsletter* and a monthly journal, *Plastic and Reconstructive Surgeon*.

American Council on Science and Health (ACSH)
1995 Broadway, Second Floor, New York, NY   10023-5860
(212) 362-7704 • fax: (212) 362-4919
e-mail: acsh@acsh.org
Web site: www.acsh.org

ACSH is a consumer education consortium concerned with, among other topics, issues related to health and disease. ACSH publishes the periodical *ACSH News* and other informational pamphlets and articles such as "Tattooing and Piercing Risks" and "Botox: 'Naturally' Wrinkle-Free."

American Psychiatric Association
1000 Wilson Blvd., Suite 1825, Arlington, VA   22209-3909
(703) 907-7300
e-mail: apa@psych.org
Web site: www.psych.org

An organization of psychiatrists dedicated to studying the nature, treatment, and prevention of mental disorders, the American Psychiatric Association helps create mental health policies, distributes information about psychiatry, and promotes psychiatric research and education. It publishes the *American Journal of Psychiatry* as well as the quarterly journal *Focus*.

American Psychological Association (APA)
750 First St. NE, Washington, DC   20002-4242
(800) 374-2721
Web site: www.apa.org

The APA is the world's largest association of psychologists. It produces numerous publications, including *Psychological Review, American Psychologist,* and the *Journal of Family Psychology*.

Association of Professional Piercers (APP)
P.O. Box 1287, Lawrence, KS   66044
(785) 841-6060

e-mail: info@safepiercing.org
Web site: www.safepiercing.org

The APP is an international non-profit association dedicated to the dissemination of vital health and safety information related to body piercing, piercers, health care providers, and the general public. The Web site features frequently asked questions about piercing, guidelines on selecting a safe piercer, and links to information on anatomy and infection control.

Canadian Mental Health Organization (CMHA)
8 King St. East, Suite 810, Toronto, ON   M5C 1B5
   Canada
(416) 484-7750 • fax: (416) 484-4617
Web site: www.cmha.ca

The Canadian Mental Health Association assists people suffering from mental illness in finding the help they need to cope with crises, regain confidence, and return to their communities, families, and jobs. Its Web site includes a linkable archive to dozens of articles on mental illness, including *Mental Illness in the Family*, *Youth and Psychosis*, and *Bipolar Disorder*.

Depression and Bipolar Support Alliance
730 N. Franklin St., Suite 501, Chicago, IL   60601-7224
(800) 826-3632 • fax: (312) 642-7243
Web site: www.dbsalliance.org

The alliance provides support and advocacy for patients with depression and bipolar disorder. It believes these disorders are biochemical in nature and that no stigmatization should be placed on the people who suffer from them. It publishes dozens of reports and brochures, including "Myths and Facts about Depression and Bipolar Disorder" and "Psychotherapy: How It Works and How It Can Help."

LifeSIGNS (Self-Injury: Guidance and Network Support)
e-mail: info@lifesigns.org.uk
Web site: www.selfharm.org

LifeSIGNS is a charitable organization dedicated to the support of all people who are affected by self-injury within the United Kingdom and beyond. Its Web site features a variety of fact sheets, a moderated peer-support message board, and a newsletter for members. The publication *LifeSIGNS Self-Injury Awareness Booklet* is available as a free download at the Web site.

National Institute of Mental Health (NIMH)
6001 Executive Blvd., Room 8184, MSC 9663
Bethesda, MD   20892-9663
(301) 443-4513 • fax: (301) 443-4279
e-mail: nimhinfo@nih.gov
Web site: www.nimh.nih.gov

The NIMH is a government agency that seeks to improve the treatment and prevention of mental illness through research in neuroscience, behavioral science, and genetics. It publishes fact sheets and booklets on several mental illnesses. The surgeon general's landmark report on mental health is available on its Web site.

National Mental Health Association (NMHA)
2000 Beauregard St., Sixth Floor, Alexandria, VA   22311
(703) 684-7722 • fax: (703) 684-5968
Web site: www.nmha.org

The association strives to promote mental health and prevent mental disorders through advocacy, education, research, and service. The NMHA publishes fact sheets, position statements, and pamphlets on mental health policy. Its Web site includes links to information on stress, mood disorders, and self-injury.

National Self-Harm Network (NSHN)
Web site: www.nshn.co.uk

The National Self-Harm Network has been a United Kingdom-based survivor-led organization since 1994. A committed campaigner for the rights of people who self-injury, its priority is to support self-harmers, survivors, and the family and friends of self-harmers. The NSHN Web site includes links to dozens of other self-harm organizations, support groups, and counseling centers.

Self Abuse Finally Ends (S.A.F.E. Alternatives)
UBH (University Behavioral Health)
2026 W. University DriveDenton, TX   76201
(800) 366-8288
e-mail: wladersafe@aol.com
Web site: www.selfinjury.com

S.A.F.E. Alternatives is a nationally recognized treatment approach, professional network, and educational resource base committed to helping self-harmers find a way out of self-injurious behavior. Its Web site offers a fact sheet on self-injury, a list of readings and resources about self-injurious behavior, as well as referrals to clinicians who have experience working with self-harmers.

Self-Injury and Related Issues (SIARI)
e-mail: jan.siari@googlemail.com
Web site: www.siari.co.uk

SIARI is the largest self-injury resource available on the World Wide Web. It aims to raise awareness about self-injury and to offer hope and support to self-injurers, their loved ones, and those who work alongside people who hurt themselves. Dozens of resources are available at this Web site, including fact sheets, articles, links to online communities and forums, and information pages such as "The Significance of Seeing the Blood" and "Dispelling Myths About Self-Injury."

Bibliography of Books

Tracy Alderman   *The Scarred Soul: Understanding and Ending Self-Inflicted Violence*. Oakland, CA: New Harbinger Publications, 1997.

Sarah J. Brecht and Judy Redheffer   *Beyond the Razor's Edge: Journey of Healing and Hope Beyond Self Injury*. Lincoln, NE: iUniverse.com, 2005.

Marissa Carney   *Stitched: A Memoir*. Frederick, MD: PublishAmerica, 2005.

Nancy N. Chen and Helen Moglen, eds.   *Bodies in the Making: Transgressions and Transformations*. Santa Cruz, CA: New Pacific Press, 2007.

Leigh Cohn   *Self Harm Behaviors and Eating Disorders*. London: Brunner-Routledge, 2004.

Robin E. Connors   *Self Injury: Psychotherapy with People Who Engage in Self-Inflicted Violence*. Lanham, MD: Jason Aronson, 2001.

Karen Conterio and Wendy Lader   *Bodily Harm: The Breakthrough Healing Program for Self-Injurers*. New York: Little, Brown, and Co., 1999.

Margo DeMello   *Bodies of Inscription: A Cultural History of the Modern Tattoo Community*. Durham, NC: Duke University Press, 2000.

Sharon Klayman Farber	*When the Body Is the Target: Self Harm, Pain and Traumatic Attachments.* Lanham, MD: Jason Aronson, 2000.
Armando R. Favazza	*Bodies Under Seige: Self-Mutilation and Body Modification in Culture and Psychiatry.* Baltimore: Johns Hopkins University Press, 1996.
Mike Featherstone	*Body Modification* (Theory, Culture, and Society Series). London: SAGE Publications, 2000.
Claudine Fox and Keith Dawson, eds.	*Deliberate Self-Harm in Adolescence.* London: Jessica Kingsley, 2004.
Fiona Gardner	*Self-Harm: A Psychotherapeutic Approach.* London: Brunner-Routledge, 2001.
Carol Groning and Ferdinand Anton	*Decorated Skins: A World Survey of Body Art.* London: Thames and Hudson, 2001.
Jane Wegscheider Hyman	*Women Living with Self Injury.* Philadelphia: Temple University Press, 1999.
Victoria Leatham	*Bloodletting: A True Story of Secrets, Self-Harm and Survival.* London: Allison and Busby, 2006.
Diana Milia	*Self-Mutilation and Art Therapy: Violent Creation.* London: Jessica Kingsley, 2000.

Arthur W. Perry and Michael F. Roizen — *Straight Talk About Cosmetic Surgery.* New Haven, CT: Yale University Press, 2007.

Alysa Phillips — *Stranger in My Skin.* Minneapolis: Word Warriors Press, 2006.

Victoria Pitts — *In the Flesh: The Cultural Politics of Body Modification.* New York: Palgrave Macmillan, 2003.

Ted Polhemus and Housk Randall — *The Customized Body.* London: Serpent's Tail, 2000.

John A. Rush — *Spiritual Tattoo: A Cultural History of Tattooing, Piercing, Scarification, Branding, and Implants.* Berkeley, CA: Frog, Ltd., 2005.

Ulrike Schmidt and Kate Davidson — *Life After Self-Harm: A Guide to the Future.* New York: Routledge, 2004.

Carolyn M. Smith and Maggie Turp — *Cutting It Out: A Journey Through Psychotherapy and Self-Harm.* London: Jessica Kingsley, 2005.

Lois W. Stern — *Sex, Lies, and Cosmetic Surgery: Things You'll Never Learn From Your Plastic Surgeon.* West Conshohocken, PA: Infinity, 2006.

Marilee Strong — *A Bright Red Scream: Self-Mutilation and the Language of Pain.* London: Virago Press Ltd., 2005.

Jan Sutton

Healing the Hurt Within: Understand Self-Injury and Self-Harm, and Heal the Emotional Wounds. Oxford: How to Books, 2005.

Maggie Turp

Hidden Self-Harm: Narratives From Psychotherapy. London: Jessica Kingsley.

V.J. Turner

Secret Scar: Uncovering and Understanding the Addiction of Self-Injury. Center City, MN: Information and Educational Services, 2002.

Barent W. Walsh

Treating Self Injury. New York: Guilford Publications, 2005.

Edward T. Welch

Self-Injury: When Pain Feels Good. Phillipsburg, PA: P & R Publishing, 2004.

Index